ENNEAGRAM
COMPANIONS

ENNEAGRAM COMPANIONS

Growing in Relationships and Spiritual Direction

SUZANNE ZUERCHER, O.S.B.

AVE MARIA PRESS　　Notre Dame, Indiana 46556

International Standard Book Number: 0-87793-510-6

Library of Congress Catalog Card Number: 93-71263

Cover and text design by Elizabeth J. French

Printed and bound in the United States of America.

Contents

Introduction

Our task is to be a guide, friend, and interpreter to
persons on their journey through their private hells
and purgatories.

Rollo May
The Cry for Myth

Spiritual direction is for people who are engaged with
their lives. That seems a simple enough concept, but it is
one I have found necessary to articulate. People seek
spiritual direction for different reasons. Some do so because their religious community either requires or suggests that its members be "in direction." Some do so
because they hear people recommend it for its benefits in
their lives, people who witness, as it were, to the value of
spiritual direction. Those who hear how helpful others
find direction may be open to the idea of it; they may
even be people for whom that expression and idea are
familiar. Nevertheless, they are not necessarily people
ready for conversion and accompaniment along that
way. They are not necessarily disciples, learners. They
may or may not be living at a level where direction is
possible and essential.

Some people never seek spiritual direction in any formal way but are nevertheless involved in the stuff of their
lives at a profound level. Such people are ready to learn,
to walk with, to be accompanied, whether they have ever
used those words or not. Gurus appear for such persons
in various places: the store, the office, the classroom, the
kitchen, the bedroom. The Spirit speaks through their days
how, when, and where the need arises.

What Is a Spiritual Director?

Very few people set out in life to be spiritual directors. In fact, those who do so might be somewhat suspect; it seems pretentious to proclaim oneself a guide on the perilous journey of conversion, of transformation. The dark nights of anguish and boredom, of terror and truth, are traveled more by necessity than choice.

Where do spiritual directors come from then? Out of my experience I have found them to be people who walk the way themselves, who walk their own way. Those around them come to observe this. They see their growing acknowledgment of hard reality, of that contemplative attitude which is the straightforward look at what is so, as Gerald May has said (May 1988).

They are people who grapple with the hard questions and learn to resist the temptation to settle for easy answers. They grow increasingly comfortable with mystery, their own and that of others, and with what some call fate, others providence. They relax into their body with its strengths and limitations. They attend to their own issues rather than flee from them into those of other people. On the other hand, their growing humble acceptance of themselves in their own humanity brings them closer to others.

Over time such people find others approaching them, not for solutions but for accompaniment. They can provide a reassuring presence along a way that we each travel essentially alone. Such presence is at times confronting, at times cajoling, at times confirming and affirming. Our needs differ at the various stages along this way. Meeting reality also offers differing experiences depending on our stance in life with its consequent view of self and the rest of the world.

The Enneagram and Direction

This is where the enneagram comes in. It can help both the guide and the traveler, the director and directee, the one in labor and the midwife, the friend of the friend, the master or mistress and the disciple on the road of life. There are a number of images besides these that focus on collaboration in this process. Accompaniment in conversion cannot be defined; at best it can be described. Multiple metaphors can prove useful in such description. None of them excludes any other. They overlap while providing different emphases.

All those metaphors mentioned above might be summarized in still another: that of a channel of God's life/Life and spirit/Spirit for the alive and inspirited person accompanied. Wherever direction occurs one thing is certain: someone is awake and listening for, if not answers, at least comments on the questions of their lives. This alert, eyesopen attitude is one of contemplation. It is an essential element in the conversion process and, therefore, the spiritual direction process.

With such a contemplative attitude a person's awareness confronts him or her despite resistance, moves despite efforts at denial, changes despite the attempt to cling to the safe, the sure, the secure. Without such an attitude things may be going on at a superficial level, but there is no radical change. There may be detached observations on one's self and experience, but there is no genuine growth and development. There may be reference to emotions, but there is neither passion nor compassion. Without plumbing the depths of life stirred up through the people and circumstances of life, no one can be walking the spiritual journey.

Let me say this again in enneagram terms. Ouspensky quotes Gurdjieff as saying we must be capable of self-observation (Ouspensky 1977). We must allow into our consciousness whatever there is to be aware of. We must grow beyond the stage of ego-development to the place where we allow into the light of consciousness more and more of what we had previously banished to the shadows of self-deception. Resistance always accompanies such a process, but even resistance is not strong enough to keep us from our reality. We begin to see "the awful truth," eventually getting used to it, and finally realizing it is not so awful after all.

Along the way to—or better, as part of—observing ourselves we need to self-remember. We need to experience genuinely, to put our story together again for ourselves, only this time with the feelings and sensations we could not bear earlier in our lives. We must let in the whole of our experience, now from a vantage point where we can bear its full impact. For example, a man who was beaten as a child may for some reason need to carry only hatred toward his father into adulthood. Later he may go back and incorporate other feelings of that time: the terror and despair of those moments, and a vague guilt or feeling that somehow those punishments must have been deserved. He may need the perspective of adulthood to have the courage to know fully the past, including the hurt that occurred because of trust and love betrayed.

Our present comes to us filtered through our past experiences. As we expand to fuller responses than the ones we might prefer or even pretend we have, we see more clearly how our past has contributed to how we respond in the here and now. We realize the past is still alive in this current moment. We understand; we "stand under" ourselves, supporting those realities we can no longer deny.

Just as we are never through observing our continuous response to succeeding moments, we are never through remembering ourselves, understanding ourselves. It is a lifelong process. We might put it another way: contemplation is never continuously experienced. The journey is never over. There are births that succeed one labor after another. We go through new and unfamiliar terrain, or over uncharted waters, again and again throughout our lives. We do so with evergrowing wisdom accumulating to each present moment.

The contemplative attitude aids our spiritual quest. It grows in us as we grow. We fight that growth in various ways, and we do so because life means frightening and demanding changes. Some of us get overly busy; some of us shut down. Some fill inner life with perceptions to avoid doing anything. Some fill outer life with tasks around connecting individuals and groups. Some shuttle back and forth looking for the one answer, which, because it is never found, never needs to be embraced. Our enneagram stance will shape our resistance.

To the extent that we resist, we will be unable to discern. We will block out one or another element leading to thorough knowing, and so lack the readiness necessary for action. Once we do find knowledge of the whole picture through our physical and immaterial being, we will have discerned as fully as we are able. Choices in our lives will follow without much effort. That is what Gurdjieff meant when he spoke of self-observation, self-remembering, and self-understanding. With these experiences we will change; without them we will remain static, safe, secure.

Of course, no one is wholly contemplative, wholly self-aware. We are all in process now and always will be because the present moment keeps changing and we keep learning to trust the moment's truth a little bit more all the time. To the extent that we do develop in this area we will discern well and choose wisely. We will be able to read the energies flowing through our perceptions, emotions, and behaviors, to deeper realizations, fewer lies, and less deception. We will find it harder to resist that which is so obviously life-giving. We will give ourselves over to life/Life, letting that life/Life carry us along. A spiritual director can help us here, supporting us and also confronting what we say is so. These two energies, the director's and the directee's, enhance the process and move it along (Assagioli 1974).

Issues Around the Topic of Spiritual Direction

One of the thorny questions around spiritual direction is how it differs from counseling and psychotherapy. I choose not to join this discussion, which I find a non-issue. Instead of putting energy into making distinctions, I will direct my remarks to the kind of relationship described above. The labels that may be applied to this accompaniment on the way of conversion are irrelevant to me. Whether it takes place in a psychologist's office, a campus minister's cubicle, over dinner, or in church is of no matter here. I join James Hillman, who has said that genuine psychology is soul-making, the evocation of the deeper self (Hillman 1975). Consequently, I wish to speak not about clinical theory or system, but about what is beneath both: an individual's encounter with the life of the self, of others, of Transcendent Being.

Thomas Malone has also spoken to this issue, saying, "The psychotherapist is one who by virtue of character development, subsequently implemented by a variety of trainings and practices, passionately attends the human spirit" (Malone 1976). Surely the spiritual director could be described the same way. Ever since Carl Jung placed human individuation in the context of the spiritual journey, both psychotherapists and spiritual directors have described themselves in terms of growth and change, of life and death. In this age of consciousness, when the human being is called to deeper, more integrated self- and other-awareness, what once seemed separate disciplines meet at the center of a person's experience.

I have already indicated many models of this kind of relationship. Whether a person looks for a guide, a director, or a scout to lead the way into unfamiliar terrain, a boatman to row across the waters of the unconscious, or a companion to hold one end of the divining rod that shows where the hidden springs of water can be found may very well depend on how he or she views life, on what constitutes his or her reality (Corcoran 1982).

Whether someone chooses to speak friend to friend in an informal way, allowing the spirit to move back and forth within and between the two persons, or whether someone hears this spirit/Spirit best through the groups and individuals who people his or her life, may well testify to the stand that person has taken toward that life. Whether one struggles through the birth process in pain, resistance and agony, held to that task by a midwife who champions, encourages, and promises that the anguish is worthwhile and ends in life, may well indicate one's enneagram place.

Roberto Assagioli has described the common thread that runs through all of the images of what we call spiritual direction. He tells us that whatever is going on with someone, the energies of two people placed on the reality of one of them is helpful. The very act of paying attention to personal experience and involving another in this process facilitates insight, movement, and change. This book is intended to assist both of the people in such relationships to see their own energies more clearly and free them for the process of spiritual direction.

One question that comes up when the enneagram is considered in the area of spiritual direction is what space one's director should be in. This question mirrors two others: Is it better to have a same or other sex director? and should a director be from a background similar to the directee? The response parallels these questions. It may be well at times to share our life with someone very like ourselves for purposes of understanding and support, assuming that person accepts his or her own reality. At other times it may be better to open up our life to someone likely to provide contrasting experience. This supports the idea of opposites and the importance of holding up another aspect of reality for broader consideration, clarity, and perspective.

The important point seems to be that someone pulled into the deep currents and whirlpools of life finds another who knows the currents and whirlpools of his or her own life. Response to fears and resistance, to anxiety and activity, to anger and resentment in ourselves is the important thing. Analogies can then be made, as I have said, to similar stirrings of the other person's depths.

Another question that comes up regarding spiritual direction is frequency. Again, there is no definitive answer. Sometimes direction is a once only experience, such as when a person walks into another's life, says or does something that profoundly changes reality, and never appears again. Sometimes direction is a weekly or monthly event. I even know of a man whose director traveled halfway around the globe once a year so they could meet.

Some people who join regularly with a person they formally or informally call their spiritual director find frequent and short encounters keep them on track. Others prefer longer meetings that help them sink deeply into their feelings. Still others sleep every night with a spiritual director who is also their spouse, or work with him or her on a daily basis. The answer to frequency cannot be separated from the model one has for spiritual direction. Therefore, as I have already noted, it may well be related to one's enneagram space.

In many ways these questions are only theoretical. The spiritual fathers and mothers have told us that when a disciple is ready a master or mistress appears (Corcoran 1982). No one will go uncompanioned on the way; someone will be there, whether a friend, a teacher, a spouse, a child, an antagonist, an employer, an author, an artist, or a pet. When individuals are ready to learn, when they are teachable, their life and those who people it will speak. The Spirit of creation will find a hearing in their hearts. Inevitably, a person feels alone and abandoned at times. Only such discomfort and pain move us beyond life as we know it. But, in fact, people learn that they are never alone in a universe in which every atom affects all other atoms. The messages of life come from unexpected sources.

However we conceive of our existence, and that existence as it relates to others, the environment, and the Divine, one thing is certain: We do so out of who we are, out of our enneagram space. I have discussed compulsive energies of the spaces and what constitutes balance and centeredness for those in differing life stances in a previous book (Zuercher 1992).

Here I focus on the ways that people bring their own journey to another in what we call spiritual direction. I also focus on the way those who find themselves accompanying others in conversion perceive and respond to their role. I address, as well, the interaction between these two people, emphasizing some of the dynamics their differences can surface.

The Purpose of This Book

"Why another book about spiritual direction?" you may ask. My answer is that applying enneagram considerations to this relationship sheds light on it. It provides some explanations for difficulties in the direction relationship— and on the reasons some people get along so easily together.

But there is a more important reason, which centers around the difference between *understanding* another's situation and *knowing* it. At best, human beings can aspire to understanding another. They can, by use of analogy, "stand under" and support the experience of someone else. They do this by listening to what a person describes as his or her feelings, perceptual connections, decisions, and actions. People place these descriptions, as well as their own observations of the unspoken messages that accompany such descriptions, alongside their own reality. They note what seems "like" or "unlike" what the person is conveying.

Those who understand may sometimes need to translate what they hear another person say. For example, the anger one person describes as a burning, blinding rage may turn another person into ice-like immobility. As people listen, they learn what each individual's words mean. They note both what is similar and dissimilar to their own truth in what the other speaks. As they attempt to make another's experience understandable to themselves by comparison and contrast, they help the speaker articulate his or her own understanding. Together they "stand under," as they see and hold more of that person's truth.

Only the individual can *know* his or her personal reality. (I use the word *know* in the biblical sense of total experience rather than as mere perceptual awareness. It implies levels of feeling and sensation as well as perception.) Working with the enneagram offers additional rationale that such is the case. Not only are no two human experiences identical, something reflective people have always insisted upon, but there are also whole groups of persons who look at life in different and sometimes opposite ways.

And they always will do so. While people can learn to listen to other experiences, they can never *know* them in the sense in which I use this word. They can understand another by analogy with, by translation into, their own vocabulary and world view. Nothing more is possible for limited human beings, who only partially reflect life/Life.

Such realization discourages some people in their desire to truly accompany another. Another response, however, is to use this realization as impetus for more careful and sensitive listening when others speak of their lives. Such people are the spiritual directors of our world, and this book is directed primarily to them and those they accompany. For them, the enneagram can serve as a powerful tool. It facilitates, first of all, self-presence; the enneagram encourages self-knowledge. Many, including myself, have written books about the enneagram with such an emphasis. It seems time to let that presence to self, which the enneagram has aided, extend to other people. By analogy, our personal insights and growth can expand to learnings about others, too.

This book is for those who know this expanded understanding is possible. It is not written only for people who see themselves involved in formal spiritual direction, but also for those who know that human beings walk together in life and can learn to do so more fully. I offer these pages as part of the tradition of the enneagram. I invite you to become involved in this process by correcting and expanding these discussions out of your own experience of the spiritual journey. What I say here is what I have personally experienced or have been told about by others. I attempt to be as faithful as I can to my own and their experience, especially when the principle of analogy beyond my personal reality needs to be applied.

Thomas Malone warns people to be careful in choosing their guides in life (Malone 1976). He cautions people to avoid both prisoners and prison guards, conformists as well as rebels. It is most important to have as a director someone aware of those compulsions that imprison the self as well as other people in one's life.

Malone adds that a gentle person makes the best guide, someone who is no longer at war with who he or she has become and who, therefore, does not need to battle with others as they have become. This gentle person is not, however, passive. He or she is able to grow and change as perceptions, feelings, and behaviors change. Malone says such an individual is never content to be content (Malone 1976). The kind of person he describes realizes the possibilities inherent in sharing the journey.

Of course, such a person recognizes, because of the level at which he or she lives life, that everyone must travel alone to deep recesses of experience as a prelude to living in community with others. Joseph Campbell tells us every hero and heroine must share the supreme ordeal, carry the cross of the Redeemer, in the silence of personal despair (Campbell 1949).

These pages are about finding a freedom that allows and encourages self and others to walk this essential and solitary path. They are also about the companionship that leads to and flows out of that freedom. I invite you to join in continuing to develop enneagram spirituality through your active participation in what follows.

Preliminary Remarks

This book discusses issues of directees and directors from two aspects. First, we will talk about some of the basic instincts of people, responses to life that are beyond immediate awareness and, therefore, beyond choice. Instincts are pre-conscious. They are present before the awake and responsive self is alert for discerning and deciding.

Early in life we begin to shape these lines of least resistance, these energies that rise up in us to which we are initially blind. As we grow in awareness, our compulsions take shape around our attempts to exaggerate what seems most natural, facile, and positive. In doing so we try to eliminate whatever would stand in the way of these instincts.

As life continues into its second phase we move beyond being creator and molder and shaper of ourselves and our image and gradually come to recognize what we have done from early childhood into young adulthood. We experience those aspects of ourselves we had hidden away and buried. Those aspects contradict what we earlier had determined to be our native contribution, our instinct. Now, in adulthood, we can no longer deny what we pushed into the darkness, into our shadow. Newly emerging aspects of ourselves reach the light of our consciousness and threaten the self-image we built up in life's earlier phase.

After a terrifying period caused by the feeling that we are somehow dying, we gradually grow more accustomed to this fuller view of ourselves. We begin to get used to aspects of ourselves we needed to be blind to earlier. Our image of being kind expands to awareness of selfishness;

our apparent calm is seen to include anxiety; our strength does not eliminate our vulnerability. In fact, the feeling of dying is understandable; the old image we created of ourselves is over and in its place a more complete, multidimensional human being is taking shape.

Over time we come to accept this more whole and truthful view of ourselves which is honestly and undeniably who we are. This attitude of humility is the basis for all genuine spirituality, because it acknowledges human limitations. It reverses the fundamental sin by which we became God in our lives, judge of our existence, and crafter of who we want to be. Humility is an honest self-appraisal that leads us to open out to include more of our reality, painful as that gesture can be. Out of such self-acceptance we open to acceptance and inclusion of others.

Whatever we name it, this evolving process constitutes our spiritual journey. It is the movement all directors worthy of the name are acquainted with in themselves. It is the way directees are traveling, if they are traveling at all. It is the road from falsehood to humility, from compulsion to contemplation, from self-idolatry to the worship of God. Various traditions name this inevitable journey the human person must take. Whether it is called conversion, enlightenment, individuation, death and resurrection, or transformation, it refers to seeing and accepting our creaturely condition with all the consequences of doing so. Spiritual direction is about human beings walking this journey together (Zuercher 1992).

The following pages consider the assistance the enneagram can give in this process. The three primary groupings, or triads, of the enneagram are addressed in turn, first as they are manifested in people who come for direction. We begin with comments that apply to all three numbers in the triad and then proceed to discuss issues specific to directees in each of the three spaces of the triad, nuancing them beyond the general description.

Next we discuss how instincts of the primary group influence spiritual directors. We note how these instincts become compulsions, which manifest themselves in the direction relationship, as well as how they constitute the contribution and strength of those directors. Besides considering how enlightened directors are both helped and hindered by their basics instincts, we discuss the trap of attempting to eliminate them along the way to wholeness. This urge to wipe out our natural instincts is a deceptive one. We need eventually to arrive at the wisdom that recognizes our gift comes from our very wound. It is awareness of instinct grown to compulsion, rather than an effort to wipe it out, which brings about such wisdom. Then directors can make choices with open eyes and greater freedom.

Eventually enlightened spiritual directors grow in awareness to admit and allow other aspects of themselves, aspects they learned to deny in the earlier period of building up instinct into compulsion. In other words, directors begin to incorporate into their innate dynamics those from other spaces on the enneagram. They do so, not by efforts that prolong the earlier, self-creating, ego phase, but by acknowledgment of what is so, by growing in contemplation. To the degree that they understand and accept who they innately are and who they have made themselves into, directors are able to accompany others in this same awareness and acceptance.

Finally, it will become evident to the reader that we are talking here about much more than formal spiritual direction relationships. Remarks that facilitate spiritual direction situations are equally applicable to human interactions of other kinds. How to listen and understand and how to respond in ways that others are able to hear and receive is information for all human interchange. Application of what is said here about spiritual direction to family life, work, and friendship relationships flows naturally from these presentations.

The 2/3/4 Triad

CHAPTER 1

Directees Who Are 2/3/4s

People who are 2/3/4s often come for spiritual direction feeling they have failed to manage their lives. Embarrassment colors, even pervades, early direction encounters with persons in these spaces. One way they handle their judgment that they have failed is to choose a friendship model for direction, something casual, perhaps never really named as direction.

I was wondering when we might get together for a chat next week. A lot's been going on for me. Maybe over lunch? I'll give you a call.

Since life for 2s is viewed in terms of helper/helpee, and since they do not want to be perceived as needing help, they are often reluctant to seek direction in a formal sense. If the environmental climate is one where direction is very acceptable, the "in" thing, 3s may be likely to "let drop" or even spread the word they are in direction, especially if they have someone as a spiritual director whose reputation is widely known. Similar are the 4s, who may subtly need to announce, at least to themselves, what sensitive and expert persons they have for directors, those able to deal with their complexity.

Direction Seen as Relationship

For all who live in this part of the enneagram it is important that directors downplay issues of relationship between director and directee. A simple yet symbolic gesture can often be helpful; to prevent continual monitoring of responses of acceptance and approval, it may be well for directors to pull their chairs alongside the directees, out of their line of vision. This lessens instinctual checking-out by focusing attention on what the directee puts out before them for both to look at.

Some directors consider it very important to be able to see the eyes and nonverbal facial and body clues of the directee. However, when relating to people in this space it is well to remember that the greater issue is one of the directee's self-presence. Compulsive attention to another in the environment militates against this. Instinctive efforts to look good in the eyes of the director will cloud over the primary purpose for 2/3/4s in direction, which is to find a situation where they can touch present experience and come to know what that feels like. The memory of such self-presence becomes a point of return outside sessions.

The Value of Immediate Experience

Directees who are 2/3/4s, in other words, need to fall deeper into immediate feelings rather than report the ones they have prepared and labeled for presentation since the last meeting. The unfinished moment just as it is here and now is where they need to be. If the direction relationship can provide such an atmosphere, 2/3/4 directees will be able to fall unreflectingly, unself-consciously into this present moment of their lives.

Continual attempts to handle things alone, to seek results, to make a finished product will give way to a here and now free from past considerations or future concerns. The tendency of 2/3/4 directees is to hurry past, to move out of moments of insight and feeling. They tend to seize immediately upon such moments in order to make use of them rather than allow them to live out their time until another moment comes to replace them.

In direction 2/3/4s believe that instead of remaining in an unfinished state of process they are obliged to show themselves and the director how well they can apply to their lives what the session has revealed. Having touched into experience that slows them down and needs to be stayed with, they often hurriedly pack up its insights and feelings to carry them away to work on by themselves. This dynamic lessens the impact of the present moment, which is their most important experience in direction.

> What I just hit on is really important. I'll think about it and get back to you with anything further next time we meet.

Those directors who find it important to summarize and conclude in order to underline the significance of a session often align themselves with their 2/3/4 directees in this compulsion. They join directees in packing up and transporting a session as a finished product.

There is little danger, however, that 2/3/4s will forget experiences that are given time to expand and deepen in direction sessions. Gradually, 2/3/4s learn to incorporate such moments into the rest of their lives. They will do the homework of seeing how their reality fits into past and future instinctively, provided the present becomes this uncommon, palpable reality.

Because this application and summary are instinctive, it is important to encourage 2/3/4s to stay in the feelings that surface in a session. Directors who are 8/9/1s may be afraid their 2/3/4 directees will be unable to come up out of their feelings to make meaning of them or continue to function. Such fear is unwarranted, however. Only giving in to present feelings will put them in touch with fuller experience. Directors who are 5/6/7s may want more information about what is going on for these directees in order to understand both the situations they describe and the persons themselves. When they do so, however, these directors tend to distract 2/3/4 directees and pull them out of a present that is difficult for them to experience in the best of circumstances.

Touching their affective life often leaves 2/3/4s un-characteristically silent. Such a silence is best left uninterrupted.

> One day I really touched into something important. I was overwhelmed and had nothing to say. After about a half hour my director quietly said, "Maybe you'd like to take this away." So I walked out. The rest of the day was a continuation of that meeting. I don't remember ever before having been so fully with myself for such a long time.

Having an Agenda

It is essential in direction with 2/3/4s to get past the stage of "How are we getting on?" to a relaxed situation in which they can pay attention to what is happening in the moment for them. To facilitate this attention the director needs to communicate that he or she has no agenda. If the director *has* an agenda, 2/3/4s often pick up that fact and spend the meeting time trying to find out what it is in order to comply with it.

Instinctive energy away from self and out into the environment will manifest itself in efforts to please the director, to help the director feel good about the session. It may also show up in summaries on the directees' part about how useful the time together has been and how much they have gotten out of the session.

If an agenda does exist, 2/3/4 directees may seem to go along with it. Meanwhile, they leave their personal reality; they decide to help directors shape the meeting rather than be faithful to themselves. This is especially true when, as directees, 2/3/4s pick up that their experience is secondary to a director's intent. Why, after all, should they search for the truth when the director has decided already where that truth is to be found? People who script life scenarios as instinctively as 2/3/4s do often respond with apparent cooperation to what they have judged to be the director's manipulation. They are no longer present at the session, no matter how things may appear.

To say this another way, 2/3/4 directees who are ready to enter the path of conversion will cover what they need to cover provided they find themselves in a free and unstructured environment. Relevant history will be accessible, conclusions will emerge, insights will flow. One might ask whether encouraging a "hands off" attitude in directors allows directees to manipulate the situation. Sometimes that may be the case. Yet it is true that this kind of atmosphere is needed for 2/3/4s to come to a deeper, affective response. Without lack of agenda or judgment they will continue to try to live up to what they perceive the director wants. Spontaneity, for which 2/3/4s continually reach, can only happen in such an atmosphere.

Given this expectation-free environment, the director can be quite active, suggesting, encouraging, expanding, questioning, as both of the participants in this search for truth and life join together. A session in which the director is forgotten is a treasured as well as rare one for 2/3/4 directees. It is in direct contrast to those in which reality is embellished, omitted, or falsified to fit perceived expectations.

"Am I being accepted or judged, merely perceived or understood?" "Is there any way you want this time to proceed?" Such questions and their answers will keep 2/3/4s, natural environment detectors, looking cooperative while absent—from self and the other—though this distance may not be obvious to either person in the relationship. It is this dynamic of non-involved interaction that causes many directors of 2/3/4s to find them superficial and boring. Knowledge of this dynamic must precede any movement toward deepening and bringing to life the direction session.

The Role of the Functions

The behavioral/activity function is prominent for 2/3/4s. Out of it many of their compulsions take shape.

The feeling function, which grounds people into present reality, is their least accessible function. Thus, living in the now, the moment, often evades them. Being at home with themselves and therefore with others is an important life task; it is their metaphor of the spiritual journey of conversion. Coming home they come to God, a Presence within them. They experience this Presence to the degree that they learn the experience of presence to themselves.

The helpful, "auxiliary" function is perception. For 2/3/4s perception frequently takes the form of reflection, a bending back on past experience, whether from years or only an hour ago. In contrast to analysis, which feels harsh and attacking and demands answers to questions and solutions to problems, reflection gently encourages and leisurely allows the past to resurface—and then ponders it. No result is sought except to know better what is so. This contemplative attitude reveals what has been hidden from 2/3/4s: their full, affective response to life.

Nor is reflection reminiscence. Reminiscence often involves daydreaming and exaggeration of some kind; it colors simple truth, painting the past as better or worse than it was. Genuine remembering involves a return to fuller perceptions, sensations, and feelings as these actually were rather than as they were limited by lack of presence at the time.

> Yesterday, as usual, I let her walk all over me. I didn't even know it till later on that evening. You know how I get sucked into going along and don't know it's happening it's so automatic. Well, I did it again.

As spiritual director for 2/3/4s it is important to distinguish between reflecting and mere reporting. The ingredient that makes the difference is that of feeling. Encouraging simple and leisurely bending back on, rather than analysis of past events allows feelings to surface. Often these feelings can be touched into only through the body/behavior function. Body sensations are readily available to 2/3/4s. This avenue to emotions is likely to be accessible upon inquiry. Not so direct experience of emotion. The question "What are you feeling?" frequently results either in mere labeling of emotions or embarrassed silence. Those who are 2/3/4s often do not know what their emotional experience is other than that they are stirred up or confused inside.

Invoking their kinesthetic sensations of feeling on or off center, of ease or dis-ease, often encourages the emotions that cause 2/3/4s these body responses. Pain or sadness or anger or fear is registered in the body, but it is inaccessible to direct awareness and insight. Physical symptoms configure emotional states for everyone, but for 2/3/4s they can sometimes be the only way to come to know emotional response. Directors who encourage attention not only to the fact of physical symptoms but also to what those symptoms are and how they represent inner states can be very helpful.

> We talked about my sore shoulders. I described how they felt and heard myself saying somewhere inside me that I'm pushing ahead of the present and that's what's making this strain. I felt my neck move back directly over my shoulders and the pain was gone right away. I try too hard and plan too much. I need to relax more.

Inquiry of the body can prevent hysteria, which is so common in the 2/3/4 stance. I speak here of hysteria in the clinical sense of psychosomatic complaints mirroring interior conflict. But the more common use of the word *hysteria*, panic often accompanied by tears of anxiety or frustration, which 2/3/4s are subject to, also applies. Free-floating anxious energy needs to find a locus so that 2/3/4s can be functional, can "survive," as they sometimes say. It does so in symptoms and complaints as well as in run-on scenarios and scripts of what might happen in the future.

Directors of such people know they must cut through this interior and exterior activity run wild. To do so is difficult, especially since 2/3/4 directees seem unable, the more anxious they become, to slow down and pay attention, to address what might lie underneath concrete experience. Surely there are better ways to spend time. There is work to do; there are responsibilities that can't be put aside. More subtly, there are the endless analyses, based on the hope that internal activity might surface reasons and solutions to current problems.

The Use of Methods in Spiritual Growth

It is dangerous to recommend methods of centering to people in this space. Methods, after all, are but another way to do something. They often lead 2/3/4s along yet another dead-end path of activity. Active imagination, whether guided or not, frequently yields nothing more than a good performance for themselves as well as their directors. Anything that suggests personal storytelling or dialogue will, the more compulsed the persons are, feed their propensity for scriptwriting.

Directors in the 8/9/1 space may find themselves emotionally affected by the memories their 2/3/4 directees recount to them. To name and touch on what these directees have named and touched on would seem to move anyone to emotional response. And yet, many times the 2/3/4 directees seem less affected than these directors, suggesting that the directees are writing a scenario rather than being led into experience.

To honor personal story through writing an autobiography or journaling about specific memories can be very helpful to 5/6/7s, who may be inclined to suggest this approach to their 2/3/4 directees. The often vivid and elaborate plots that result when 2/3/4s do take up this suggestion may lack the substantial feeling that emotion would provide.

Dream work, too, may deteriorate to retelling the dream stories, while the question "What can I do about all of this?" underlies the account. Gestalt techniques of identifying with objects and speaking as though one were one's hand or pencil or some other concrete object may yield interesting dialogues but often little emotional movement for 2/3/4s. Nothing is touched, nothing shifts.

Perhaps the one "method" that 2/3/4s can find helpful is the focusing technique formulated by Eugene Gendlin (Gendlin 1978). His approach to centering, to the felt sense, invokes the body for response, asks the body to speak, as it were, of its experience. After placing this request to one's organism a person merely waits without further activity. If 2/3/4s can be faithful to Gendlin's directions, they can often move to self-presence. His method offers something to do in its steps, but it is a something to do that quiets and allows the body to instruct.

Since 2/3/4s are always looking ahead in life, they often cannot see what is currently going on. To bring their gaze to the colors, the objects, and the persons in this moment helps bring them to the here and now. Adding the more primitive senses to the visual one intensifies being in the moment. Consciously focusing on sensations maximizes use of the body's avenues of awareness. Tones of people's voices as well as their words, the tastes and smells in the environment and in the memories they point back to can enrich these realities.

Above all, touch, both given and received, can lead to being in touch with self. It is important that such touches are not grasping and clinging ones of desperate anxiety, but free ones of choice beyond this compulsion. Learning the difference between a tight, hungry hug and allowing one's hands to teach one about personal reality is important, especially for 2s.

> I picked up her letter and held it in my hands. I noticed how rough and hard the paper was. It felt as hard as the words she'd written on it. I felt they were rubbing me raw inside.

When offering suggestions to 2/3/4s it is important to remember that they will usually appear to be willing, even eager, to jump through any hoops they suspect you may be holding up for them. They want to be successfully in touch, to do well, to create a good impression, to go away feeling the session has not failed and you are pleased with and in harmony with them and it. In this way they will feel satisfied with themselves. They may not even know this is so, that they are fulfilling your agenda and sometimes nothing more. You as director may sense, when looking back at your meeting, that much went on at a level of activity while little went on at any depth.

When the session gets stuck at this level of doing, it is necessary to put aside any methods except suggesting to directees that they invoke their bodies here and now. What do they see in this moment? What do they hear in their own and your voice? What do your postures say? What do they experience right now in their bodies, and what is that about for them? Then move away with them to wait without attempting to answer any of the questions, allowing the body to give its own reply.

It may be well here to highlight that we are speaking of 2/3/4s in compulsion. To the degree that directees in this space are aware and accepting of this instinct toward activity and so are freer from it, various approaches to interiority become appropriate. These might include dream work, dialoguing, active imagination, graphic art, or any number of other methods. Still, the instinct to become entrapped described here will be present, and in stress and crisis 2/3/4 directees will return to it.

What Constitutes Guilt for 2/3/4s?

All people, no matter from what vantage point they look out at life, experience guilt. What particular feel does the guilt of 2/3/4s have? It consistently includes the behavioral function and revolves around the theme of relationship with others. People in this space assume responsibility for whatever goes on in the environment. There should be no need, no conflict; no one should feel alone or left out or disconnected from relationship. If anyone does feel this way, the fault rests with the 2/3/4. He or she should have done more—been more aware of situations, of people, of dynamics, of needs. Guilt at a more superficial level often involves image. What will people say? What will they think? How will I look?

I was having some guilt over sexually acting out with Mike. I imagined myself before God in prayer one day and was surprised I was okay with it all. I knew God saw everything anyway and I felt his acceptance. Then why was I feeling guilty, I asked myself. Who wouldn't accept my way of life? All of a sudden my mother appeared in my imagination and I knew she was the one. She wouldn't approve. It wasn't about God at all.

The implication here is that guilt relates to activity, to something I did or failed to do, to something I did wrong. As 2/3/4s become more contemplative, as they move further along in the conversion process, they develop beyond this single view of seeing life merely in terms of their activity function. They find more simple presence. They learn to be rather than to do and recognize that activity often covers over inadequacy at the level of their very existence. It is no longer that they do not *do* what is enough or right; instead *they* are not enough or right. Guilt is no longer about what they have done but about who they have failed to be, taken up as they have been with the superficial and external.

Appalling shame follows. Often this shocking awareness is what brings 2/3/4s to a place of quiet where they find no answer, where they are overwhelmed with the evil they have perpetrated against their own being. They also come to realize that they have treated others with that same insensitivity manifested toward themselves. Once 2/3/4s arrive at this level, they will be better able to utilize the direction experience. They will still have a tendency, however, to return to action as a cover for incompetency and inadequacy. This cycle from doing to being and back to doing is what constitutes the feeling of continual activity directors experience with 2/3/4 directees, even those who are enlightened.

The Issue of Independence

Another dynamic that comes up when relating to 2/3/4s is a curious sense of both independence from and dependence on others for validation and affirmation. On the one hand 2/3/4s hold on to control of their own lives and experience; on the other, they seem to need people more than other types do, especially in the area of approval of who they are. Strong expressions of opinion and apparently confident action contribute to the first impression, one of independence. The dynamic from which this sureness of expression comes needs to be described more fully so that it can be understood for what it is. Firm assertions often do not manifest the definitive decisions they seem to.

Since for 2/3/4s life is about having some response, they see themselves as needing to be ready for action at all times. In order to be ready they constantly evaluate, assess, judge, and set priorities for both interior and outer reality. Such appraisal leads to decision-making, the necessary preface to action. Once they arrive at their decisions, 2/3/4s can begin to do something about what they have observed and assessed. They sound firm, finished, and confident enough to act. They are, but they are also not as unchangeable as they may sound.

While 8/9/1s often enter into argument around what they hear as this 2/3/4 conviction, and 5/6/7s tend to back away from these people who have no questions and are actively making things happen, it is well to remember what is really going on in this dynamic. Others' input can easily modify their attitudes and outcomes, especially if this input reveals disapproval or opposition. Because 2/3/4s arrived at their decisions and actions quickly, they are able to change them on the basis of response from others. Because investment is minimal, it is not hard to adjust or even discard their decisions.

Directors of 2/3/4s need to explore what appears to be conviction, probing its affective components, if there are any. Finding the depth of the feeling around apparent convictions shows how deep they are. Because they have the same instinct, 2/3/4 directors may more readily understand and be less surprised at sudden changes and shifts in their 2/3/4 directees.

There is only so much that can be said in general about this or any of the other basic enneagram triads. Themes and issues differ from one number to another in this stance. We will now look at each space in an effort to speak more specifically, and therefore helpfully, about knowing and responding to others who live there.

CHAPTER 2

The 2 Directee

A word that often comes up around the 2 dynamic is *rescuer*. Rescuing takes various forms in 2s' relationships and, of course, shows up in spiritual direction. Feeling bad about one's self, feeling lonely and cut off, are situations 2s see as needing to be changed. There are frequent interior conversations that 2s carry on with themselves about the importance of their thinking more positively, of getting out of negative moods. They accuse themselves when they feel resentful or angry toward others. Such inner dialogues are reminiscent of those that 1s have, but they are toned down from a scolding energy to a quieter one of advice-giving.

Other people also ought to have this positive attitude, and affirming others seems to 2s a way to help. They affirm by removing people, including themselves, from experiences that do not, in their eyes, seem to serve any purpose. Such tactics show up in direction sessions in the form of flattering remarks to the director, often made at moments of tension during the session. Such remarks are aimed at keeping the director from pursuing some difficult issue. Compliments of this kind serve two purposes. They assure the director that the 2 directee is pleased with what is going on; they also indicate indirectly and often unconsciously just how uncomfortable the directee is willing to get.

This dynamic is one reason why directors find it hard to cut through superficiality, reporting, and wordiness with their 2 directees. This complimentary style of avoidance is probably best dealt with by pointing out to the 2 what has just taken place, leaving comments on that observation for the directee to make. Many times 2s are not aware of what they are doing and having it described helps them recognize their fear of acknowledging the unpleasant.

A shift away from moving into feelings sometimes comes in the form of solicitude for the director, who then takes over the focus of the session. Mention of whether the director is tired or ill, concerns around the director's family members, or comments about some interest the director has previously manifested is inserted. This happens either to replace the subject of the session or to fill uncomfortable silence. Humor can also bring about this shift. A light touch in the form of a clever expression or amusing incident diverts from the pain and sadness 2s fear looking at. There is often a sense that they feel a poverty of interior resources to meet their own or other people's darkness; just laugh and it will go away.

Many problems 2s encounter in relationship are traceable to their tendency to give advice. As 2 directees discuss conflicts with people in their lives, it may be well to listen for indications that they have rushed in on someone uninvited. Their words and behaviors may have been designed to let people know how they ought to be, to feel, to behave. They are, after all, only trying to help. Their good intentions ought to be obvious to anyone with sensitivity and a kindly attitude, or so it seems to them. They are confused and hurt by others' less than positive reactions to this solicitude.

> I can't understand how my husband can just leave the children to fend for themselves, and I tell him so. They're great kids and they need us, both of us. I wonder what would happen if nobody ever came to their defense when they needed it.

This taking care of others in their world is so basic to 2s that it is difficult for them to see it as anything other than desirable. One description catches these dynamics humorously: "She is a person who has given herself for others. You can tell those others by their hunted expressions." As 2s become more self-aware, more contemplative, they learn to see these hunted expressions on the faces of recipients of their kindness and advice.

They learn to distinguish the difference between Augustine's recommendation to love and do what you will and doing what you want in the name of love, the way Riso describes this compulsion (Riso 1987). Their totally virtuous self-perception is unmasked, revealing the fierce independence and need to control relationships that lies beneath.

All of these dynamics are resistances that hold the director off, unconscious and instinctive as they often are. The approach for the director of 2s is just to lift up the experience for observation and to leave all suspicion of judgment aside; that is, the director can utilize their independence by leaving them alone to make the choice of facing and meeting what they are doing to themselves. They need to see how they are abandoning themselves at the level of their feelings and needs.

When 2s do see, they need the director simply to be there. When they can no longer deny what they have been doing, they will probably want to run away from this discovery. What they considered to define their reality—their advice and service—they now unveil as a way out of looking at life. The director must stand by and not join in any kind of denial or condemnation; rather, the director's presence models self-presence.

Through other people 2s come to God, and through other people's words they hear God speak. Seeing honesty coupled with no judgment on the director's part, 2s meet an accepting Divinity. Love is no longer at the level of an ego task, a building up of positive self-image; it moves gradually to the removing of boundaries of self-deception.

> When I look into your eyes I see all that sadness I don't want to admit I have. I can't look at you. You show me how I'm not really listening and hearing myself.

A frequent stance for 2s is that of suffering martyr: people sin against me, not I sin against them. After all, I care even when nobody else does. Much of the anger of 2s clusters around the fact that their good intentions go unacknowledged and unappreciated. Besides pain and sadness, they deny anger and aggression. When their hostile feelings are acknowledged and accepted, 2s usually have a bright, if brief, blaze of temper. When anger is denied, a reproachful hurt colors relationships, including the relationship of spiritual direction.

> Sometimes I wonder whether you have any idea just how necessary it is for me to do all these things I'm doing. It's not like I can just stop. If I didn't get involved nobody would. Nobody seems to care. You keep asking me to look at my own needs, but how can I?

Overextension not only breeds this kind of reproachful righteousness, but it also weaves into other 2 issues. When loneliness and emptiness surface as themes, 2s frequently come to the realization that, in trying to be all things to all people, they have forced their time with others into hurried, non-present encounters. Exhaustion results and indicates their personal limitation. If that fails to deliver a message, psychosomatic complaints force them to slow down; their body rebels. All of this emphasizes their inability to determine their own needs. Something outside them says the no they cannot choose to say.

In compulsion 2s often apologize. They seem to be sorry, not only for what they aren't doing, but for who they are not. They have, after all, broken down in the name of love, as Riso puts it. That ought to be enough, but they find it is not. If they are brave enough and intent enough on the path of honesty and conversion, they eventually realize the lie that precipitated their compulsion. Not only have they deceived others with protestations of care, they have done all of this to hide how they really feel about themselves. Their compulsion has helped them escape the profound fear of personal deficiency. They taste their lack of being, which they covered over by doing.

The director at this point must continue to stay with the 2 directee and must communicate a confidence that something of being exists. This communication probably best happens not by affirming words, but by patiently waiting through the resistance 2s express by running off again and again into activity, as they did in the past.

Affirmation, as every 2 comes to know, can be easily offered. Twos eventually learn to distrust it in themselves and, consequently, in others. However, if the director does not give up on them and moves on to what 2s see as happier and more fruitful encounters by comparison with what they have to offer, perhaps they can also learn to stay with their experience. Thus the pain of seeing their cowardice and flight play itself out over and over again can be endured and, eventually, accepted.

CHAPTER 3

The 3 Directee

The constantly recurring theme for 3s is success. They need to feel successful; they must look "together" and confident in the eyes of others. To this end 3s sacrifice vulnerability. Limitation means that there are flaws in what they are doing, in their products, outcomes, results. Worse still, these flaws indicate deeper ones at the level of being. Their interior selves are a mystery to 3s. Clues to a 3's identity come from external behaviors. Imperfect actions indicate failure on the part of this unknown and evasive being from which the 3's activity must flow.

People in the 3 space are anxious that they might be pitying themselves. At times 3s are frightened that disparaging and depressing attitudes toward themselves will paralyze them, making them unable to produce up to par. If they were to let in misgivings about themselves they would be less functional. Too much concern over their own incompetency and inadequacy might freeze them into inactivity.

Another reason for 3s' fear about self-pity is the realization that, if they are not competent and capable—their frequent descriptive words for themselves—that is a sign they are unable to manage their existence by themselves. Indeed, if they cannot master life, that points out a deficiency that both eludes and haunts them. It shows up a deficiency at the core of their interior selves. At that core 3s feel they live with a stranger.

This person they do not know but who dwells within has more actual existence for 3s than it has for 2s, who

45

question the very reality of a self apart from their helping activity and sometimes describe their interior as a hollow emptiness. Threes usually acknowledge an interior exists, and even feel they are somehow in relation to it as to another person. Still, they feel little connection with this interior self. At best, it is an unknown who they discover through observing exterior behavior. At worst, it is a caged monster who may cause unpredictable moods or alienating bursts of anger or evasion.

This interior sometimes manifests itself as unmanageable. It remains, when they are in compulsion, a distant sort of acquaintance rather than an intimate friend. They wonder how to measure and evaluate this self who inhabits their interior. They fear that if they were to spend too much time in pursuit of relationship with themselves, outer work would go undone. There would be nothing concrete on which to base self-assessment. They would never know whether they were making any progress. This view affects 3s' attitude toward spiritual direction, where they instinctively watch for outcomes or conclusions on which to evaluate either themselves or the direction relationship.

Direction can cause 3s much anxiety; they often feel like blind people, attempting to know without being able to see. It is precisely "feeling around" for their kinesthetic experience that can help acquaint them with their interior. When they become aware of tightness in their body, a sense of relaxation, centeredness, agitation, they find a way to move from analytic seeing to experiential understanding. It is this trusting to their sense of interior touch that leads them to their affective life.

One problem 3s often talk about when they describe relationships with others is how frequently people fail to come through for them. Such comments usually mean that others are not carrying out the plans and directions they have set for them. Threes often give out jobs for other people to do, assuming they will be happy to carry out orders. When persons are not pleased to do so and reveal their displeasure by noncompliance, 3s are surprised and angry.

Why don't people pull themselves together and accomplish? Ill health or negative feelings are no excuse. Since 3s themselves keep on amid hardship, since they keep functioning no matter how adverse circumstances may prove to be, why are others unable to do so? This question is a variation of the one other 2/3/4s ask concerning the inability of people to keep functioning no matter how adverse the situation.

> I asked them to take care of that meeting, but as usual they didn't. Nothing came off the way we'd decided. The agenda wasn't out on time with the materials that were needed. And then they got huffy with me. I'm the one who has a reason to be angry.

Guilt for 3s has a flavor of "I must have done something wrong, and I wonder what it is?" Not being in touch with their interior and coming from a stance where they feel themselves to be the center of attention, they are anxious others may be discovering something they themselves cannot see. If, indeed, they feel they have not done anything wrong, then they fear their interpersonal difficulty may stem from something left undone.

With 3s, as with other 2/3/4s, guilt is tied up with relationships and the vague sense of some inadequate presence to others, which hints at lack of presence to self. What they do is identified with who they are. To criticize any activity of theirs is to say, in effect, that their existence is not worthwhile.

As they become more aware of their shadow, 3s are forced to admit how strong a theme deception is in their lives. The first person they deceive is themselves, because they need to see themselves in so positive a light. They are always capable, functional, in charge, or so they need to consider themselves in the early years of their lives. This is the time when they are building their egos and the self-image they project for other people. It is by this self-image they want to be known. Reality adjusts to fit that image, which means that their limitations have to be hidden away.

Enlightenment, a growing contemplative attitude, conversion, or however one chooses to label the process of coming to fuller awareness and self-acceptance, brings this dynamic of deception to light. Initially, 3s tend to flip over from deception to a ruthless search for authenticity. They pride themselves on being straightforward and confronting both interiorly and with others. The energy of this scrupulous honesty is harsh. It holds an anger that attacks both the self and the other people one confronts. Actually, it is merely the substitution of another deceptive image to replace the former one of social adaptability. This new role testifies to straightforward courage. And it is a role, an imitation of the honesty they see in others.

> I just said to him, "Look here. I know what you're trying to do, so just admit it." You should have seen his face. He's not used to meeting up with somebody so willing to call his bluff.

One clue to the fact that this apparent authenticity is yet another pose, a substitute role, is the fact that 3s are so conscious of it and need to let people know the level of insight they have arrived at. This "Hey, look at me" quality in what 3s do and say indicates the superficial level at which they are touching into their feeling experiences. When they lose the nearly constant audience and speak to themselves unobserved by imaginary others, including the director, they are at a place of interior movement and change.

Riso (1987) has called 3s the most narcissistic of the spaces. It is around the role-playing of honesty just described that this narcissism can often be observed.

Threes are more self-image centered than the other spaces, more taken up with the reflection of themselves. In the myth Narcissus was fascinated by his face mirrored in the water. This does not mean that 3s are necessarily more selfish than other people, who may be preoccupied with some other aspects of their reality, such as their self-preservation, safety, or moral rectitude.

Another factor that contributes to a sense of narcissism in 3s is a propensity in some of them to say aloud whatever is going on inside. The director may have a running commentary on every self-preoccupation that passes through the 3's mind, while other spaces often keep their interior ruminations to themselves. This dynamic makes 3s obvious targets, fair game for assessments of self-centeredness from anyone looking on and listening.

People who relate to 3s often label them braggarts. In reality, 3s are probably only trying to define for themselves and their listener or observer where they fit in the external scheme of things. By placing themselves in relationship to others around them they tell the inner and outer audience who they are. If the people they speak of as their friends and associates are outstanding in any way, it says to them that they, too, are outstanding by association. The depth of their insecurity is often in direct proportion to their recounting of successful relationships and affirming stories.

This basic lack of confidence is perhaps the greatest obstacle 3s need to climb over before they can relax into themselves as they actually are, before they can be honest, before they can begin to move into conversion. An atmosphere of unconditional positive regard might seem to hold what 3s need in direction. It is often, at least, what they say they need.

In reality, an atmosphere where the director all but disappears is frequently not only a more helpful but also a more honest message. It would hardly be honest for a director to affirm everything in a 3 directee, nor is this what 3s need. What happens when 3s do forget their director? They no longer have to perform as a competent directee might perform. They turn their gaze inside instead of concerning themselves with how they appear to the director. They give up trying to figure out whether the director wants something specific from them. Instead, they simply ask what is so, what their personal experience actually is.

Assuming such an invisible role is not to underestimate what directors of 3s provide for them. Directors need to be focused and present somewhere in the background, ready to handle fears about those unknown but suspected monsters that might rise out of interior darkness at any moment. That is all the director ultimately has to offer—standing by while 3s face what they fear might prove too overwhelming. It is this fear of not being able to function that keeps them from looking within.

At best, directors provide assurance to 3 directees that they will be able to get up on their feet again no matter how tumultuous the session has been; they will be able to walk out and pick up their lives. When directors do provide such support, they facilitate what is most needed in this space: genuine authenticity. In humble honesty 3s find the strength to see the truth, to accept it, and to allow it to shape their lives.

CHAPTER 4

The 4 Directee

Where 4s are concerned, the issue of self-accusation dominates relationship. Riso has captured better than anyone else this aspect of the 4's personality. It may not appear externally, because efforts to maintain connections with people cause 4s to cover over their basic sense of being unredeemable. Despair is at the heart of life for 4s. There is no hope that any relationship will be genuine, or, if it is, will survive time. The reason all relationships fail is, they believe, because they themselves lack something essential. That something is, of course, genuine and concrete experience, though it takes 4s a long time to realize that fact. For ordinary reality 4s substitute exaggerated emotionality. They do so in an effort to hold onto a sense both of their own meaning and also their relationships with others. Their appraisal of the impossibility of an enduring relationship is often an accurate one. This unreal quality in 4s does, in fact, drive people away.

Like all 2/3/4s, people in the 4 space are certain that relationship with other people is the only value in living. That this is their top priority is not obvious either to themselves or to those on the outside looking in; 4s appear more self-sufficient and distant than others in this general area of the enneagram. Really, however, relationships are as vital to them as they are to 2s and 3s. The conviction that relationships are impossible for them, however, causes them alternately to reach out and to hold themselves off from others.

I cling, but only on the inside. I never want others to know how much I need them because it might put some obligation on them as far as I'm concerned. And, ultimately, I don't want any expectations myself. I don't want to let myself hope that relationship can endure, because I know I'll be disappointed.

Their panoramic view of beginnings and endings, of births and deaths, shows up in several 4 issues. Everything is seen as either the waxing or waning of the life/death cycle. As a result, everything is laden with meaning and significance. All experience takes on symbolic dimensions, contributing to either the ecstasy or tragedy of life. Nothing is merely of the moment; everything has ramifications far beyond itself. For 4s, reality actually feels as intense as those outside them hear them describe.

Another manifestation of this panoramic view is the absolutizing 4s do around their feelings and behaviors. Against a background of life/death issues it is easy to fall into extremes of all or nothing, of total surrender or total independence, of supreme happiness or complete despair. The struggle of the 4 in direction is to look neither toward the past nor the future, but straight ahead at present reality. The inability to do so is, indeed, very painful for 4s. It is important for directors somehow to appreciate that fact and communicate understanding of this fear of the present that 4s have.

Frequently the style of 4s in direction is to summarize their feeling journey in a statement about the meaning they have derived from it. As 5s offer a pithy remark on their perceptions, 4s present brief philosophical axioms or conclusions that often sound peaceful and wise. This being the case, directors of 4s may see them as aloof and emotionless, an attitude 4s strive for because it seems to promise the state of harmony, interior as well as exterior, so important to them. It is hard for 4s to admit raw emotion to themselves, let alone share it with someone else. Consequently, directors of 4s may feel detached from them and their experience. When this happens it is usually because 4s have successfully distanced themselves from the impact of reality, choosing a vague, melancholy summary as substitute.

All that childhood stuff left me lonely, but it also taught me I had to stand alone. It's the real source of my independence today. I know I can take just about anything and survive it. All that early pain fits into the picture of who I've become.

Such summarizing of life's real fears and angers, anxieties and frustrations, is part of the honing of existence that 4s instinctively do. They are often called artists, not because of any special artistic talent, but because they shape and form all of life. Relationships become a problem when others do not respond as planned and scripted; anger that might destroy an encounter is carefully examined and couched in as accurate and reasonable a way as possible. The intent of crafting anger is to avoid any irrational outburst that might lead to questioning its justification. Fours need to be prepared for encounters. To that end, and to reinforce a sense of security, 4s tend to invite people into their world rather than to go out into the environment of other people. In that way they feel more in charge of shaping what happens.

Fours need to realize that making life an artifact is the reason they fall into despair. Life holds situations of miscommunication and misunderstanding, on their side and that of other people. They will never find the harmonious world they seek. They will never find the peaceful, rhythmic flow of their interior life as a constant, either.

Usually, when this realization comes to them, 4s turn their shaping of experience toward forming a spontaneous attitude to life. The ungrounded, "free spirited" 4 often expresses this phase. In reality this posture is no more free than previous ones. Eventually 4s who continue into honesty are forced into that despair of ever being able to make their beautiful world or to resist the effort to do so. Out of that despair they are forced to self-acceptance and relaxation with how things really are.

When listening to 4s, directors sometimes hear what sounds like amorality. Really, 4s are intensely moral, as they are intense about everything in their lives. They have stringent moral criteria, to which they are committed. In essence, whatever is growthful and life-giving demands their embrace and motivates their scrupulous search for genuine emotional experience.

Riso says that 4s fear something is fundamentally wrong with them, something they cannot put their finger on (Riso 1987). What feels wrong is often that false and unreasonable expectation of a rhythmic and flowing world inside and outside themselves. To create this beauty they ask themselves how to behave so that problems will never occur again. It is around their less than harmonious behavior that their guilt occurs. Any irritated, frustrated, or angry response from another signals to them lack of grace and beauty, which they have caused. It is this need for rhythmic flow that manifests itself in careful choice of clothing appropriate to the occasion, in a beautiful journal, or a direction session that begins well, develops, and comes to resolution.

Despite these efforts toward beauty, especially in the self, 4s are repulsed by their raw feelings and often by their body and its behaviors. As they become more enlightened, 4s realize that their self-disgust leads them to push other people away. They may then come to encourage others to stay with them through this compulsive phase until once again they see themselves as desirable.

Whether or not 4s actually articulate such a request, their directors need to communicate that they intend to stay through 4s' experience of an ugliness that so frightens them that it leads them to disgust and despair. It is also important, however, that those who direct 4s refuse to play a part in the scenario these directees create. Walking the line between staying with and refusing to be manipulated is not easy.

Understanding the 4 dynamic and communicating that understanding to the directee is, in the final analysis, what counts. It also prevents 4 directees from playing into their compulsion to create yet another perfectly formed relationship. Then, when all efforts fail and they fall again into despair, 4s can learn that the director's continued presence contradicts their hopelessness. When this attitude is reached, direction can prove fruitful for 4s.

CHAPTER 5

The 2/3/4 Director

We will now consider the dynamics we have discussed above as these influence spiritual directors. The reader will note that this section on the 2/3/4 director is slightly longer than that for directors in other triads. This is because this section includes background information that applies to all spaces. The message is the same, of course. We bring to all of our relationships who we are. It might be well, however, to look at these life themes from another vantage point. How do the vices and virtues we have been talking about play themselves out in those who direct others?

Anxiety

Directors in this 2/3/4 space are influenced by high anxiety. This anxious quality characterizes their particular kind of insensitivity. The word insensitivity implies that the senses do not pick up what is present; something of reality is not taken in and processed for awareness and response. For directors in these spaces it is feelings other than anxiety that most frequently elude them. Other emotions are covered over with agitation around future plans, scenarios, and goals. Focused ahead, 2/3/4 directors may bypass genuine present feelings in both themselves and their directees.

One result of anxiety is that 2/3/4 directors find it hard to keep from activity of one kind or another. They often want to respond before someone is finished speaking, to finish others' sentences, to supply words when there is a pause. They tend to jump to conclusions rather than stay with a process. They may be inappropriately self-revelatory in an effort to connect with directees. They may fill silences with words rather than allow others time for quiet self-presence. Anxiety may also manifest itself in a need to make things happen for their directees rather than leaving the responsibility and readiness to them.

Roles

Besides outer behaviors, 2/3/4 directors may get caught in interior analysis of what their directees are trying to communicate. They sometimes pull directees into this analysis and away from their feeling state. Such inappropriate and ill-timed words and behaviors are present to the extent that anxiety is present. They constitute the particular kind of insensitivity to which 2/3/4 directors are prone. Remarks that do not fit the situation and blindness to feelings give the impression of hardness and coldness, manipulation and invasion, superficiality and inattention; these describe 2/3/4 directors in compulsion.

Probably more than any other directors, those who are 2/3/4s are aware of their spiritual director role. They usually have an inner imagination of what that role requires of them, especially if they are 2s who see themselves cast as helper and the directee as one who needs help. As much as they strive to encourage mutuality and friendly connectedness, a subtle hierarchy of one who gives and one who needs frequently emerges. People constantly observe themselves in this part of the enneagram. They assess how they are doing as directors, compare themselves to others, look to directees for indications of how things are going, and consequently either feel good about themselves or become paralyzed by their inefficiency.

Because of this 2/3/4 tendency to ask "How am I doing?" supervision of 2/3/4s is often difficult. Supervisors collude with 2/3/4 supervisees' own interior observer, assessor, and analyzer, who already looms too large in their learning process. How well 2/3/4s are really doing as spiritual directors is probably never accurately assessed in the supervision situation.

> I'm just not myself when I know I'm being taped for supervision. I freeze up and feel like I'm on stage under the lights. I just can't come out with anything remotely spontaneous. When I'm alone with my directees I can forget everything but them and things are fine, very natural.

Affirmation

Somewhere in the world view of every 2/3/4 is the desire that people be helped to feel good about themselves; there exists, as well, some expectation that such security is attainable and is what all people are working toward and can actually achieve. While it is true that an atmosphere of support and care forms the basis of any good direction relationship, it does not follow that affirming and complimentary remarks necessarily contribute to that accepting environment. Directors in the 2/3/4 space gradually realize that the good intentions behind their affirmations can backfire in a number of ways.

Possibly nothing is more alienating to a directee than to be refused ownership of feelings. When directors talk people out of loneliness or sadness, self-disgust or alienation, they only contribute to those feelings because they are not accepting their directees' reality. Directors who try to push directees into feeling better about themselves distract them not only from what they are trying to communicate, but also from where they are emotionally.

> You know, when you say these things about being so frightened I find myself unable to take them in. You're really so strong and calm in the face of everything. I'm not the only one who sees you that way. It must be so. Can you plug into that strength right now to balance out your fear?

Affirmation often serves no purpose. If the directee is already in a centered place which is peaceful and positive, there is no need for the director to underline the obvious; to do so only interferes with self-presence and movement in the session. If the directee is in a state of anguish, unable to accept self or some aspect of self, compliments only sound hollow and empty and often result in a tangential conversation about who has the accurate perception, the director or directee. At best this slows down movement in the session, and at worst it creates distance between the two.

Over-Connecting

The major concern for 2/3/4s is to establish and maintain contact with other people. Directors in this space need to watch for their compulsions around this instinct. Some, as already described, advise directees how they should feel. Others move immediately to recommend to directees what they need to do and how to go about doing it. While their perceptions may be correct and even helpful at times, 2/3/4 directors can move directees out of emotional presence to themselves and into action prematurely.

Still other directors, in order to encourage directees and be supportive of them, inappropriately share their own history, acquaintances, problems, and any number of other personal areas. Sometimes such exchanges have a flavor of one-up-manship, therefore diminishing the directees' experience by implying how much more fully they have known the same problem. While this is often intended to give confidence to directees, it can have the opposite effect.

> I know how hard it must have been for you to grow
> up without a father. I can empathize with you; both
> of my parents died when I was very young and I only
> knew aunts and uncles, no parent at all. That was a
> painful sort of childhood.

What compulsed 2/3/4s consider the most important aspect of existence, the need to connect, shows up in their personal lives and affects them as spiritual directors. It leads to breadth rather than depth of encounter both with self and others; it results in quantity rather than quality of relationship. No one can continuously nurture and attend to as many relationships as 2/3/4s might feel they need to. In compulsion they become exhausted by efforts to forge stronger bonds with everybody in their environment. Such exhaustion often goes unnoticed until it manifests itself in illness, the body's way of talking back about its needs.

Lack of punctuality can become a problem. People who relate to 2/3/4s may have trouble counting on their arriving on time for appointments. Who knows how many interactions surprised them on their way to this one previously scheduled? When they do arrive, they are sometimes emotionally unavailable, worn out, tired, and distracted from responding to so many situations along the way.

Such unavailability to self and to significant others causes 2/3/4 directors to listen poorly and fail to be present with directees here and now. One dynamic plays into another, and the anxiety that leads to over-connecting combines with fatigue, limiting the effectiveness of encounters. The richness of their own interior is sacrificed and their presence as directors is also impoverished. They substitute quality of presence for efforts and plans. The more they do so, the more they feed their compulsion and the less the actual dynamics of the session are able to emerge. Spontaneity goes out to the degree that control and goal-orientation enter.

Over-Responsibility

Compulsed 2/3/4 directors are absorbed in their roles and descriptions of how good directors function. They measure themselves on agendas accomplished and objectives reached. Simple presence with directees when these directees are present to themselves is lost among activities. When it is, compulsed 2/3/4 directors often suspect something is wrong—even at times what is wrong—but they are on an accelerating spiral hard to stop. They want reassurance and appreciation, at least some sort of feedback, but often fear to hear all is not well.

As a consequence, they keep on going, hoping the outcomes will make up for their growing sense that all is not right in their direction relationships. If they can stop for some honest comments or questions, they may break through this mounting anxious activity and come back to feelings in the moment. But that takes courage, a willingness to risk hearing about their inadequacies. When it does take place, however, they can begin to relax and give over responsibility to their directees. They learn to listen more in order to facilitate the directees' listening to self.

As 2/3/4 directors grow more enlightened, they are frequently amazed at how unable they are to touch into their own emotional life. They are especially chagrined to see how they collude with 2/3/4 directees in maintaining superficial conversation—reporting and planning with little depth of emotion. They may seriously question whether they ought to be engaged as spiritual directors, as well they may question. If such insight leads to honesty and humility, if it forces them to give up their efforts in despair, it can become motivation for greater personal affective living. Then, in their direction sessions they will return authority to directees where it belongs.

> Last fall I was in a really bad space. I couldn't do anything at all in my own life or in my sessions with my directees. Now I'm amazed to find that the people I've been seeing are to a person going back to last fall as the time they found my help most significant. I guess what I did was get out of their way because I felt too helpless to do anything else.

Taking Care of vs. *Caring For*

Perhaps the most important distinction 2/3/4 directors need to make is between taking care of a person, doing something for a person, and having genuine care. Care is a multi-dimensional response. At times it means honest communication in the form of confrontation. Sometimes it means leaving directees alone and untouched, physically or psychically, so as not to interfere with their search for their own experience. Other times it may be consistent, conscious efforts at maintaining contact as a testimony of companionship. These are only some of the faces of care. Care always responds to what is going on in the changing moments of relationship. Therefore it demands that one be focused in the present.

Taking care of, on the other hand, is superficial. It may involve various actions, but they all hold the feeling of "doing something for" the other person. They include a sense of carrying the other along rather than walking with the other as that person travels his or her own path. Taking care of others makes them dependent. It involves seducing needy people, who can then hand over responsibility for their lives to someone else. It is also being seduced by the lazy, who get 2/3/4 directors to do their work for them. Because it is either being seduced or seducing, it is a game, and a game that 2/3/4 directors are prone to play.

Taking care of often combines with the natural impatience of 2/3/4s. They tend to push for decision and action so things will start happening and results can be seen and tallied. Such manifestation of anxiety is in direct contrast to allowing things to emerge in the life rhythm of the directee. Consciously, 2/3/4s, because they live in the social triad of the enneagram, want to work together with others toward goals. Unconsciously, they can be so driven to make things happen that they take over. When that happens they tend to move directees along, out of their feelings and into insights around these and actions out of them.

Because 2/3/4 directors tend to bypass their own emotions, they may miss others' feelings, too. They skip over affective components of experience and push directees, as they push themselves, into doing something. While 4 directors may find obvious manipulation repulsive, they still may attempt to control in more subtle ways.

Fear of Disconnecting

Such dynamics lead to disturbed and conflictual relationships between directors and directees. The greatest fear 2/3/4s have is breaking bonds with people. Upset in their relationships with their directees makes them fear these relationships may be destroyed. Were that to happen, the ordered view of life in which everyone is either smoothly connected or desirous of and working toward such connection, would be lost.

In the face of this fear, compulsed 2/3/4 directors try to remove its cause. In order that difficulties either will not occur at all or else will pass by quickly, they often rescue, compliment, and affirm directees. They may try to talk them out of their anger, sadness, or whatever blocks the relationship. Even enlightened directors who can readily admit their compulsions in this area can get caught into making efforts that flow out of fear to sever or disturb relationship.

As directors, 2/3/4s tend to absorb the experience of their directees, not by taking on their emotions, but by making things happen for them and doing for them what they think needs doing. They may try to make life better, to relieve difficulties, and to resolve others' problems.

They can also be possessive of their directees. Since the distinction between self and accomplishment is hard for 2/3/4s to make, they often strive to assure their own worth by making sure that their directees are progressing. They stand up for directees at supervisory assessments or in other arenas where motives or actions of these directees are being questioned. Criticism of directees amounts to criticism of themselves. They can be fierce champions of "their own" in obvious or subtle ways, depending on their individual space.

> I don't like to hear you so hard on Joe. If you knew a little more of his struggle, I think you'd have a better grasp on what's going on with him. His response really does fit the situation if you listen to his reasons for doing what he's doing. He's made a lot of progress that might not be obvious if you haven't been working closely with him.

Standing up for directees often includes reference to how well the director knows them, how the director alone is privy to information about their personal lives. Alluding to the depth and importance of their relationships with others serves as a testimony of how well the director interacts with people. It reinforces the director's image to himself or herself and to others.

Healthy directees are not receptive to having 2/3/4 directors manage their lives. If the directees are 5/6/7s, they will probably feel overwhelmed and invaded. Their response is withdrawal in one or another form. If they are 8/9/1s, they will probably become angry or at least mildly annoyed and stand firm, holding off efforts on their directors' part to take over either passively or actively. When directees are other 2/3/4s, there may be an even stronger reaction depending on how accepting these directees are of their own shadow. If they can forgive themselves for manipulating other people's lives, they can also forgive their 2/3/4 directors; if they are negative and denying of this dynamic in themselves, they will project that self-disgust onto directors who manipulate them.

Whatever the response to this dynamic in their direction relationships, 2/3/4 directors need consciously to face up to it. It takes maturity and insight to address problems of manipulation and move beyond them.

The Ability to Adapt

Instinctive adjusting to people and the environment is another characteristic of 2/3/4s. Such adaptation can include modifying ideas, feelings, and behaviors. When compulsive, it blinds them to the dynamic. They lose touch with their interior life. What 2/3/4/s often call the search for authenticity centers around this dynamic.

At some point in the conversion process 2/3/4s learn to inquire of themselves what response is their own. They turn to personal, authentic experience as the source of their reality and inner authority. When they do so they let go of the exaggerated instinct to look outside for truth and, instead, encourage the balance of inner and outer.

> I always want to know how things are for everybody in my environment. While I'm trying to find out I never think about asking the same about myself. My motive for looking at others, if I'm honest, is to figure out what my response to them should be. That's all that counts, not what I think or feel or want.

Instinctive adaptation in 2/3/4 directors becomes compulsive and problematic. It shows up in the tendency to adjust to the level of relating—be it superficial or substantial—their directees choose. It simply takes without question the subject matter the directee brings as agenda for a session. Adaptation also appears when 2/3/4 directors turn away from objective data if such information would call for confrontation.

More subtly, perhaps, it shows up in a director's complete self-forgetfulness. Some directors actually cultivate losing themselves in what is going on with their directees. Being so present to directees that they walk in their shoes, as it were, can result in losing touch with information their training and skill could offer.

It is important, then, for 2/3/4 directors to balance a sense of themselves with sensitivity to directees in their sessions together. When they learn to do that, they find an important natural gift of accompanying another that is beyond the exaggeration of their social instinct. Then, moving out to the directee becomes facilitative rather than compulsive.

Being able to enter into anther person's world, to look out from his or her stance and view of life, is one of the major contributions of 2/3/4 directors and one of the characteristics of their personal style of direction. It needs the balance, as does their entire spiritual life, of an interiority that draws them to inquire of their own experience. It draws them inward to honor their own response and to make available additional data for full presence in the direction relationship.

Also related to this theme of outer emphasis is the 2/3/4 appreciation of every person's uniqueness. Instead of generalizing from data or judging from initial impressions, 2/3/4 directors, when enlightened, take people in their individuality. They become little inclined to apply stock assessments of people or rush to conclusions before hearing them out. Since they focus intently on the other, 2/3/4 directors are predisposed to listen for nuance as they grow more sensitive. Such listening presupposes that they listen to themselves and are familiar with their own instincts and compulsions. It goes without saying that they have come to know and respect the parameters of their own limitation and gift.

When they can accept their own experience, 2/3/4 directors learn not to deny similar experience in directees. They can accept without threat whatever the directee presents, even when this may be personally frightening to them. At best disruption and at worst destruction are feared to result from anger in the 2/3/4 world. Directors in this space may, therefore, consciously filter out expressions of frustration, rage, or resentment, which are some ways anger manifests itself.

Needed Skills

In subtle ways 2/3/4 directors may overlook or avoid their directees' angry emotions, whether these are directed at them or at other people or circumstances. They may also advise directees out of these feelings, sometimes almost arguing or cajoling them away. They may also try to affirm their directees out of feelings.

> I know you've really had a bad time with him, but just remember how gifted you are. He's probably jealous; he knows he can't hold a candle to you. You're on top here if you can only see it.

One of the most difficult skills for 2/3/4 directors to learn is confrontation. For 2/3/4s, confrontation often appears harsh and uncaring, something they never want to be. It can look to them like the opposite of acceptance, which they always want to offer directees. As a help in dealing with confrontation, 2/3/4 directors do well to view it as part of what constitutes bonding and connecting. In reality, to confront another is to offer the truth of one's assessment and response.

How the director perceives, feels, physically reacts, assesses, or otherwise relates to a directee's reality is communication to offer. While it constitutes the director's authentic response, it is only that, and can be modified and corrected. This kind of confrontation invites discussion and the kind of interaction that moves a session along rather than blocks it in an adversarial way. Linking confrontation with the desire for authenticity can sometimes give 2/3/4 directors the courage needed to reveal their honest response, even when it holds potential for conflict.

Contributions from the Behavioral Function

The more enlightened 2/3/4 directors become, the more they are aware of how instinctively they use their behavioral function. They analyze, organize, set goals, make plans, and write scripts on the inside. They carry out those plans, bring about conclusions, make things happen on the outside. While this instinct surely leads to some of the 2/3/4 compulsion, it also holds opportunities for assistance in the direction relationship.

Once known, this propensity to action of some kind can help directees who do not have the same instinct. When offered consciously rather than from compulsion, ways to decide and plan, to work with others, to focus on outcomes, to take into account the customs and mores of the group can contribute to directees' movement. When it includes ways of helping directees invoke the energy of their emotions, it can assist them to appropriate decisions and action. Such informed discernment frequently moves directees who might tend to overlook their activity function to respond out of the energy of their feelings.

Because they value and feel at home in the concrete world, 2/3/4 directors are comfortable addressing useful, pragmatic issues. They can be helpful in grounding experiences for people not so inclined. They are able to lead those who tend to become bogged down among options to organize these into priorities. They often assist directees who get overwhelmed with emotion to separate from these feelings. Once these directees can distinguish between themselves and their affect they see it as only part rather than all of who they are. Less threatened, directees can begin to address these emotions and move beyond inertia.

Because 2/3/4 directors are prone to comparisons and competition, they tend to examine their own dynamics alongside those of people in the other spaces. When they do so they often judge themselves wanting. Their natural gift of doing seems less worthwhile than that of perception or emotion. It strikes them as more superficial. While such comparison is part of their instinct, it can interfere with their functioning as directors. It can also have the good effect of motivating them to greater interiority.

When they diminish the value of their behavioral instinct, 2/3/4 directors may tend to withhold its contribution from their directees. They may assume a more passive stance. They may allow directees to flounder when assistance from them as to how to proceed could prove beneficial. This is a delicate call. On the one hand they know their ability to be seduced into taking over responsibility for people's lives. On the other, they have information that could contribute to freedom of choice and movement for directees.

The way to distinguish whether compulsion is operating at any given moment comes from self-awareness, the experience of freedom or its lack. If they can offer suggestions without a need for their directees to accept them, they can be assured manipulation is not going on. If their body is relaxed and at ease, they are not compulsed. Compulsion and gift come from the same instinctual source. One gives a feeling of dis-ease and the other flows easily. The more contemplative the director, the more he or she will be able to read the kinesthetic message as to whether compulsion is operating.

Responding in the Present Moment

The call in every person's spiritual journey is to live fully the present moment, all of reality we creatures in time ever know. This experience of here and now requires that 2/3/4s stop looking in a linear fashion from past to future, from side to side. Instead, they need to focus straight ahead. When they do this in a direction session they attend to as much of their own and the directee's reality as is possible. An enriched, better informed present is the result.

They find that the moment has various dimensions: feelings to be plumbed, body responses to be noted, insights to be explored in themselves and the other. As they learn to read reality moment by moment they are able to balance at the same time both their own and the directee's truth with increasing facility. They inform their actions with growing accuracy of perception and genuine feeling.

Awareness of the present leads to sensitivity for directees and their needs. From a compulsive urge to touch, to hug, to invade verbally, to impose advice, 2/3/4 directors are more able to distinguish when their directees need to be alone. They leave directees to sift and sort experience for themselves. They allow them to endure an aloneness that necessarily precedes self-companionship. As enlightened directors, 2/3/4s have come to discover the difference between being in touch with directees emotionally and moving too much into their physical and psychic space. They have learned for themselves the value of tasting the sinfulness of compulsions. They have come to understand this experience as the essential prelude to casting themselves onto the power of life/Life, for only then can they allow the Divine, that power over which they have no control, to shape them.

When 2/3/4 directors realize how they swing from a compulsive clinging to an equally compulsive self-sufficiency, neither extreme can deceive and therefore control them any longer. Whether their independence takes on the 2 flavor of "I don't need you," the 3 declaration of "I'll do it myself," or the 4 isolation of "You don't understand," it loses its power when it becomes conscious. When it does, they have more freedom to enter helpfully into the direction relationship with no demand on directees.

When they learn that by staying in the moment a person finds all the future with which it is possible to be in touch, 2/3/4 directors find their anxiety lessens. They can let go of plans about how to proceed in direction relationships, where to move, what to do next. The more enlightened they become the more easily they will be able to encourage directees to do the same. On their own journey 2/3/4 directors have to learn to shy away from looking to the past and future for clues to the present. After they have realized the trap in this regard they can make use of that very tendency to assist others who need such perspective. While it is important that they not exaggerate the instinct in themselves, they need to remember other spaces can often use more of it. They can learn not to dismiss their own dynamics out of fear of compulsion, but rather to use them in dealing with others unlike themselves.

Another area in which 2/3/4 directors need to remember to offer others the methods toward interiority that may be traps for themselves is that of personal remembering. Working with memories and history is an essential part of the conversion process. For 2/3/4s themselves it is probably best to reweave their personal story by focusing on present responses. The feelings, perceptions, images, and attitudes found in the moment when followed back yield information about earlier reality. People respond in the present out of accumulated experience. Since 2/3/4s are inclined to live in the past and future, methods that focus on memory can entrap them. Looking for clues to past experience in the here-and-now response can help them stay in the moment.

For directees in other spaces it may prove helpful consciously to write an autobiography or keep a regular journal; those in the other triads are less likely than 2/3/4s to find such an activity deteriorating into either a dramatic production or a mere recounting of events without feeling. Being able to be in the present moment with their directees will tell 2/3/4 directors what methods of addressing memories are appropriate. They may well learn to suggest approaches to others that do not facilitate work with their own personal history.

Seeing the Whole of Life

Balanced and centered people, whatever their enneagram number, have learned to let in more and more reality, to become contemplative. When 2/3/4 directors move toward greater centeredness they do so because they find an interior energy as real as is the compulsive thrust of their energy outward. The alternating depressed and enthusiastic reactions of 2/3/4s are often similar to manic depressive swings. Such extreme swings are caused by refusal to let in authentic emotional experience. The denial of feelings, learned early in life as a protective strategy, becomes less extreme as a more total and honest life develops.

This movement back and forth between hyped and depressed energy comes to be recognized for what it really is, an effort to cover over real feelings which might threaten positive self-image. Kindness and generosity, control and equanimity cannot always color a person's affective climate. But early in life 2/3/4s expect they should and push away any reaction that would contradict that expectation. Submerging instinctual responses leads them to alternate feelings of depression or flight from depression (mania).

Enlightened 2/3/4 directors have learned not to trust their extreme reactions and the cosmic and absolute conclusions that flow from them, whether positive or negative. They put off evaluation and decision at times of either extreme enthusiasm or lethargy. Greater equilibrium comes in direct proportion to the ability to admit whatever they are genuinely feeling, whether it is appropriate to act out of those feelings or not. They learn to distinguish the difference between admitting what is going on affectively and expressing it in action.

Quietism

They also learn to distrust a blank, interior lifelessness that sometimes masquerades as quiet and centeredness. Time teaches 2/3/4s to admit and allow their real feelings. They learn how doing so brings them more fully to themselves. The result is a genuine quiet that does not come from denial but from honesty. It is a quiet that flows out of emotion owned and given time to be. When they learn what they do to themselves to create false serenity, they can be helpful in watching for quietism in their directees.

In their role as directors 2/3/4s develop the ability to distinguish centeredness from an emotionless state. They can then help directees unmask deceptions that result in quietism. Such deceptions may take the form of interior or exterior laziness, a sleeping through life rather than addressing it. They may also involve perceptual preoccupations that allow some directees to detach from their experience and the decisions and choices that flow from them.

2/3/4s' View of Spirituality

The greatest evidence of 2/3/4s' native contribution to spirituality becomes more and more clear as they come to balance and wholeness. It is the ability to see life as one piece without boundaries of secular or spiritual. From this perspective nothing can be godless. Prayer becomes simply living and breathing; it is not contained in any place and time. The holiness of human life is everywhere; translation into spiritual—let alone religious—terms is unimportant.

Such an attitude in 2/3/4 directors can be disconcerting to directees who do not share it either because it is not their natural world perspective or because they are in compulsion. Directees may come to wonder what spiritual direction is all about for 2/3/4 directors. They may find their directors unable to attend to their prayer and spiritual life as distinct from the rest of reality.

Indeed, 2/3/4 directors can sometimes appear, if not amoral, at least "areligious." Their theology is sometimes so blended with other disciplines as to have no distinction, no parameters in itself. Other 2/3/4s who come to them for direction are often relieved to find themselves free from having to hold off the spiritual aspect of their life from its other aspects. They need not report on their prayer life, but on their life as a whole. People from other spaces, however, may be disconcerted with their 2/3/4 directors' approach. It is not only not their own view, it is not their way to conversion.

It is important that 2/3/4 directors realize these differences. Their attitude may, indeed, enlighten the struggles of others who are unlike themselves; it can contain a perspective of reality that enlarges how these others look at life. However, it will do so through the lens of a spirituality not instinctive to these directees.

Directors who are 2/3/4s need to be aware of any impatience toward others for whom rules and laws as well as struggles between what is secular and spiritual hold great significance. As directors, they need, as always, to acknowledge their own response and allow and take seriously the other person's.

> It gets tedious for me when I hear people talking about their worry and guilt over what the church says. Then I try by analogy to remind myself how it feels to get so concerned over what people will think about me. In some ways those are my laws.

As 2/3/4 directors come to accept and address their own issues, they will be able to assist others to admit and address theirs, whether these are similar or very different ones. When they know their own fears, traps, embarrassment, deception, and evil, they will be able to open to those of others. By analogy, directors in all of the triads have this same challenge. When directors accept it, whatever their enneagram space may be, they grow as much as their directees do.

The 5/6/7 Triad

CHAPTER 6

Directees Who Are 5/6/7s

We now move to another of the three basic spaces. When we do so we need to change focus, to put ourselves into another world. People here look out at life very differently from those we have been speaking about in the previous section. What is the world view of 5/6/7s? What is their stance toward life? We will begin with some general characteristics and move, as we did with the 2/3/4s, to considerations unique to each of the numbers. We will then speak about the traps and the contributions of directors who are in these spaces, remembering that both limitation and giftedness come from the same instinct.

Hyperperception

Those who are 5/6/7s have a natural propensity to pick up what is in the environment, to "see" what is going on around them. They are also inclined to take this information inside and order it. This instinct is both a natural ability and, when overly relied on, a compulsion. It leads 5/6/7s to misread what living is about. They are inclined to conclude that they know all there is to know once they have taken in and observed objective data. It is as though a wrapped package were delivered to their door and they merely attended to the way it appeared on the outside without opening it to discover its inner contents.

When 5/6/7s come for direction, therefore, they are inclined to present the facts of what is going on in their lives. They often do so with a detached quality, observing themselves and others with noninvolvement, at least from an emotional standpoint. They watch their situation and are interested in it, but may still seem somehow distant from what they speak about.

They do have energy focused around seeing what is so and seeking for meaning out of it. This energy may arise from a need to control life, a need people in all spaces experience. Indeed, whatever urgency is ours, it leads to the creation of the image we offer ourselves and others in the first part of our lives. For 5/6/7s, mastery is seen as coming from taking in all the perceptions available. This results, at best, in an overly objective approach to life. In compulsion, it causes a detached observance of one's self, a discounting of the importance of one's complete and personal experience, emotional response, history, and activity. This emphasis on perceived meaning can wring out life and leave it dry and withered.

> Joe told me about how his paralyzed mother sat for hours beside her dying husband, unable to speak, to act, to phone for help, to reach out to him. I teared up as I felt that woman's anguish. But Joe didn't. He told it all as though it was something he'd read about in the paper, not something that his mother had endured. In a way, his detachment was more shocking than the situation he'd described. I asked him whether he'd ever felt what his mother had gone through. His answer revealed he didn't know quite what I meant.

It is important in direction genuinely and fully to remember, to put back all the pieces of an experience, with 5/6/7 directees. The substance of life events has layers of feeling. When the search for meaning and answers clouds fullness of experience on multiple levels—actions, words, emotions—life is narrowed and deprived. The pulsing passion of joy and pain and sadness, of fear and anger, and all the other nuances of feeling fills out life and pulls a person into its flow. All but the most compulsed 5/6/7 directees know this at some level. They look for directors, as well as friends, whom they trust can help engage them in their lives.

As 5/6/7s look for directors, they also search for ones who will consider them important enough to listen to and spend time with. It is hard for some 5/6/7s to think they can be of any importance to others, that others will find them interesting enough to hear them out. In their efforts to look for how situations and concepts fit together and how they themselves fit into reality, they often need to wander through a myriad of perceptions, ideas, and insights along the way.

What is happening in their lives and where they find themselves in relation to those happenings may take a long time for 5/6/7 directees to determine. When they do come to that determination, it is often the result of a private and interior perceptual pursuit. Directors who have the patience to wait out the search and the skill to facilitate it are the ones who gain the trust of 5/6/7 directees.

Where 2/3/4s spend their energies creating consonance with people, 5/6/7s are more focused on resounding with the environment, creation, and reality itself, both interior and exterior. They gradually feel into it, finding a home there rather than being an outsider and lost. As 5/6/7 directees move into conversion along these steps toward union with what is, directors can assist the journey by encouraging them to note and allow their feelings about what is going on. How 5/6/7 directees experience their emotions is a question they may not instinctively ask. To attend to it invokes the auxiliary or helping function, which for 5/6/7s is their feeling function.

The Anonymous I

The efforts toward remaining anonymous, part of the withdrawal of 5/6/7s, are characteristic of all three numbers in this basic space. It is more apparent at the 5 place, but exists as well, despite their more outgoing quality, for 6s and 7s. While they do appear quite friendly, there still is in these latter two spaces an interior privacy, even detachment, a desire to remain at a distance and hidden. An ambivalence occurs when 5/6/7s find that they are indeed inconspicuous, that they have achieved that invisibility they wanted to have at least as an option for themselves.

As is true for all human beings, 5/6/7 directees find it important to be taken into account and paid attention to. The message of desire for privacy they give out can create a feeling of loss and separation, which no one wants all the time. Directees who are 5/6/7s often present issues around this search for intimacy. They look for directors who will be sensitive to this dynamic and who gently will help them to address it in friendship and in the direction relationship as well.

One way anonymity and hiddenness are manifested is in 5/6/7s' use of third person statements. They will sometimes quote other people to communicate what they themselves think, usually others they consider expert and well-informed in the matter under consideration. Sometimes these third person references take the form of "They say" or "It is said." In some cases they may even refer to themselves as though they were observing their own lives from outside.

> Mary has a lot of things to bring to this session, Bob. She's had a rough week and she could hardly get up the energy to get here. It took nearly everything in her to get her job done. Anyway, here she is; I guess she'll start with just that, the job, with how things have been going with the boss.

Before venturing out with many of their own communications, 5/6/7 directees test directors. They try to assess what their directors think about issues they present as well as who they are as persons. They often watch and wait for directors to take the initiative or else offer items of information for directors to respond to.

This can be a disconcerting dynamic for directors who wish to remain in a facilitative role, responding to the movement the directee experiences and indicates. It can also lead some directors to question whether 5/6/7 directees are looking for their director's Achilles' heel, for some place to fault them. In reality, it is more likely a dynamic on the part of 5/6/7s to find out whether the director is truly interested in them—which means, first of all, in their perceptual gatherings. Will the director want to hear about their ambivalence and data collection? Will he or she be willing to stay on through the time it takes to communicate what may seem to both of them to be vast interior wanderings?

To conserve time for themselves and their directors, 5/6/7s often skip over details which, while very important to them, they fear may bore their directors. Could anyone else care about the ideas, let alone the person, of someone as inconsequential as they sometimes perceive themselves to be? Manifestations of impatience, boredom, and inattention they experience from others around what they themselves find very engaging provide data for the validity of such a question. The fact that people may wander off mentally, or even physically, while they are talking or may introduce an irrelevant topic in the midst of their communication testifies to the rightness of questioning the interest of others.

Another concern for 5/6/7s may come from the frequent experience of doing and thinking for other people. Insights and evaluations of their own easily become the property of persons with whom they share them. When others listen attentively to them they may become suspicious, as they are inclined to be anyway, and conclude people are using them to avoid having to do their own interior work.

The cautious, tentative, slow-growing assessment of 5/6/7 directees demonstrates trust-building around such issues. When they find directors who indeed are interested in them, not just in their ideas and concepts, they can become quite verbal and articulate. Perhaps nothing means more to 5/6/7 directees than for directors to recall and make connections between information previously shared and elements in their present conversation. This experience testifies that the director, too, is at this moment holding their experience in mind; the director is seeing patterns and meaning in their lives and can be trusted as paying attention, taking them seriously, and valuing everything they say.

Such an experience may well be the final test that opens 5/6/7 directees to freer sharing. When that happens, their careful, sometimes sparse verbalization can change to a flood of words as they put out what until that moment had only been thought. Hearing themselves speak can be frightening; it can also give their perceptions a concreteness important for discerning their validity.

Fear as a Dynamic

There hardly ever exists discussion about 5/6/7s that does not include talk about fear. What is it that 5/6/7s fear? Many things, of course. Among them is fear that they do not yet know enough, have enough information. Effects of this fear can be seen in concern over finishing—or beginning—projects, coming to decision and action. There is also fear that, if they do not trust their own authority and make their own decisions, others will do so for them; they will have become victims because of other people's initiative and their own hesitation.

There is fear of chaos, of lack of ordered meaning, or at least of their own ability to find the meaning that does exist. Such concern sometimes leads to the concentration on how things could be, on how reality fits together, which characterizes this space.

While 5/6/7s are usually quite conscious of their fears, they may not be as aware of anxiety, their most buried emotion. Anxiety is probably experienced and spoken of as apprehension around what is unknown. It is frequently distinguishable from fear by the fact that it involves some sort of activity: humming or whistling, making things neat and orderly, learning more and more about something. In their fear and anxiety, sometimes experienced as one and the same thing, they look for directors whom they describe as being trustworthy. These are people whose knowledge and experience 5/6/7s see as reliable.

They are also people with whom they can share their phantom fears. When they do admit these, 5/6/7s often find that these fears dissipate or at least are lessened. Because of their shame at being concerned over seemingly small matters, they hesitate to let others know about them. This hiding, of course, buries their fears away, and what frightens them tends to grow. The amount of fear in proportion to the stimulus becomes stronger and seems to them to be even more ridiculous; they grow even more reluctant to express it. Given this dynamic, the problem of communicating fear only intensifies.

Trustworthy directors must be people who, when 5/6/7s unwrap their prepared packages of communication, are seen as willing to help prevent these from getting lost. As inner meanderings increase, they can grow into mazes with dead ends and circuitous avenues that sometimes arrive back at the starting point. Not knowing where or how to go in this interior world is not only hard to admit because it seems so foolish, it feels frighteningly unsafe. Directors need to demonstrate willingness to walk with 5/6/7 directees through the labyrinth, compulsive as it may be, before their suggestions toward how to move beyond or beneath it will even be entertained.

> Sometimes when I get ahead of rather than walk alongside him I feel as though we begin to go off on different paths. He gets this lost look on his face, which I used to call resistance, but which now I see more as confusion. When I give up forging ahead to some in-

sight or conclusion, our paths merge again. Sometimes that takes lots of patience on my part. I'd like to get on with it, but I've learned when I do I lose him.

Fears of 5/6/7s include appearing unwise or looking, as this director observes, confused or illogical. When they are in such a state they often become acutely aware of a naivete that makes them vulnerable to deception, invasion, or analysis. They fear their director may prove to be disloyal, that after all their opening up they may still be put aside or betrayed. The child they often feel themselves to be, having ventured forth, now stands unprotected.

Small wonder that, given this concern, 5/6/7s lead in conversations with what they are sure of. It is easy to understand the reason they tend to offer prepared and processed reality. It seems sensible that they are inclined to offer small portions of information and couch these in the form of testing questions, thus keeping their private persons safely and detachedly hidden. Sensitive directors not only will be aware of these dynamics, they will be patient through the time of gradual testing until trust is established.

Withdrawal

Where do 5/6/7 directees go when they withdraw? Always to a place they consider safe. For 5s that may well be into their observations of people and situations. From a watching vantage point they feel more sure of what is going on and learn who deserves their confidence and respect. Sixes often pull away into their belief systems. There, with others who think as they do, they find strength in the loyalty of friendly associating. Sevens, who move into ideas, plans, and possibilities as a form of withdrawal, risk being deceived by their own fantasies. They need someone who won't take advantage of their suggestibility but who will be excited and interested in the things that excite and interest them even while pointing out fallacies and exaggerations.

Such forms of withdrawal are sometimes intended as self-protection. At other times it is simply that 5/6/7s don't think to reveal what they know. Even their style of speaking manifests the conscious effort it can take to open their interior world to another. They not only speak summarily at times, they may do so haltingly, leaving loopholes for quick escape in the middle of an exchange.

Directors can facilitate communication and movement by helping their 5/6/7 directees unpack, tease out, and further reveal their experience. In the effort to stay present to them, directors honor their directees' experience and model how they themselves need to honor it. Concrete, specific events 5/6/7 directees describe, often in great detail, need to be looked at for elements of feeling as well as mere data. The personal story of how events affected and changed them are considerations directors need to draw attention to if their 5/6/7 directees do not do so for themselves. The emphasis needs to change from narration of the facts of life, whether past or current, to affective experience of life events.

Those who are 5/6/7s often look as though everything makes sense to them when in fact it does not. They are inclined to tell others the part of their experience they have worked through, keeping the unfinished to themselves. Generalizations, whether terse or elaborately developed, often cover over areas of confusion where they feel unsafe. What has already been figured out will be, if not the only, at least the first communication. What is still in chaos and mess seems worthless to put out because it is only a partial solution. The order and fit is what 5/6/7s want to see and what they think is worth the telling.

What they have learned is the important thing, not themselves struggling to make sense of reality. They do not like this struggle to know, and they want it to be over. Why would you want to spend time in such a state any more than they would? As directors choose to be with them in process, 5/6/7 directees begin to choose this also. They move their emphasis from gathering information to personal response. At this juncture they begin to appreciate and respect a fuller dimension of who they are, their joy and pain and struggle.

All of this happens when 5/6/7 directees are ready, of course, and not before. Gradually they move beyond telling the director only what they think when asked how they feel. Skillful and caring directors learn to listen for unspoken questions, concerns, and emotions beneath the facts 5/6/7s communicate. Such directors will be subtle in both inquiries and challenges. They will not rip open the prepared packages of information but discreetly invite rather than demand directees to untie the strings.

Directees who are 5/6/7s are especially sensitive to pressure, pushing, and meddling, to having their lives taken over by those they may see as more passionate, strong, or competent. They often need time to ensure that their directors do not belong to such a group, will not draw them out and then drop them. As directees, 5/6/7s need to know that if they do move into process their directors will not leave them to be lost in their chaotic and unfinished reality.

> It takes me quite a long time to feel comfortable with somebody so I can open up to them. That's not only true in any relationship taken as a whole, but I seem to need to do it every time I meet that person. I spend time checking out whether a person is listening or not, whether they're in a hurry or on some other wave-length than mine. Every time I go to direction I go through this process at least a little, even though I've met with the same director for a long time. I seem to need that assurance over and over again.

The importance of focus and presence on the director's side is essential, no matter what the enneagram space of a directee. In relationship to 5/6/7 directees it takes the form of attentive holding of what even these directees think seems insignificant. In fact, what looks unimportant when presented, what is offered in an unassuming, unembellished, unadorned manner, may hold great importance. Asking 5/6/7s to enlarge on it while respecting their word choice and encouraging them to expand it by further description becomes an invitational and encouraging help. As they hear their own articulations they can listen to and respect deeper levels of their own experience. Without such an approach, directors can indeed find sessions with 5/6/7 directees non-engaging; often this is because their 5/6/7 directees are themselves not engaged in their lives, or if they are, cannot imagine the director would want to be.

The Place of the Affective Function

It is a fact that 5/6/7s need to move from perception about their reality to feelings around it in order to grow and change. What are some ways directors can help this to occur? We have already mentioned encouraging 5/6/7s to enlarge on personal experiences beneath the words they use. To do this demands patient listening with long periods that may have little to show in terms of movement.

It sometimes helps when directors share experiences similar to those their 5/6/7 directees describe in order to confirm these directees' reality. If, instead, this is done for the purpose of connecting with them, it will probably be seen as invasive; these directees are not there, after all, primarily for relationship with the director, but to determine the reality of their own lives.

It is important for directors of 5/6/7s to be conscious of the trap of putting everything into words for their directees, a temptation especially for 2/3/4 directors, who sometimes grow uncomfortable in extended silence. This temptation might be particularly present when working with 5s, but it holds true for the other two spaces in this triad as well.

Just because 5/6/7s do not respond verbally does not mean they have not heard what has been said, have failed to take in suggestions, have missed the import of the communication. In fact, they may have been deeply touched and need time to move from the lostness of so many new considerations to an integration of them. Sometimes it helps 5/6/7s when a director shares observations about their body responses. The body is not instinctively taken into account by people in these spaces. Noting and remarking on qualities of voice, body trembling, posture, and expressions in the eyes can help them include these perceptions and acknowledge the emotions manifested through their body.

People in these spaces have a hard time discerning among options. They frequently are unable to move from accumulated perceptions to the level of feelings that propels a person into action. This is the case because they often cannot feel where their energy really is, where their life flow is pulling them toward further growth.

The experience of energy, which is a physiological phenomenon, is experienced in the body or not at all. The kinesthetic sense mediates this energy into awareness, which is another way of saying that one's life thrust is experienced through the body. Therefore, besides noting observations of exterior bodily behavior, directors of 5/6/7s do well to suggest to their directees that they inquire of their body's inner response to data: tightness or relaxation, fatigue or refreshment, rest or agitation, conclusion or unfinishedness.

When 5/6/7s, who see themselves as objective and factual, hear themselves described as judgmental, they often register surprise. In fact, their judgment is not the instinctive "I like" or "I don't like" prejudgment of the 8/9/1s, but rather a more detached kind. Emotionless assessment of something either as right or wrong, fitting or not fitting, seems to them to be merely in the realm of objective observation. It often comes across otherwise, however.

> I just know this is right, no matter what she says. She may think she saw the whole picture, but she was wrong and I feel I needed to let her know. She doesn't need to get huffy about it. I'm only telling her how it is, pointing out what it is that's missing in her evaluation of things. I experience a duty to do this.

Anger often gives 5/6/7s the impetus they need to act on their own behalf or to accomplish what needs doing. Many times they experience anger around a sense of victimization, of feeling taken advantage of, an attitude common in this space. As they become more converted they begin to realize how they have allowed this victimization to happen, how their own dynamics of holding themselves out of the stream of life make them prone to takeover by other people. When they see how this happens they become angry less with others and more with themselves. Sometimes this anger turns in and they feel helpless and depressed; sometimes it leads to asserting their own authority over decisions and actions affecting them.

Another source of anger occurs around other people—often, though not exclusively, authority figures—who do not do what 5/6/7s consider right. This is the pharisaical kind of anger described as prevalent in this space. It can look at times like the moral judgments of the 1, but it holds the flavor of legalism; the 5/6/7 emphasis is on whether others keep the rules and do what is right and fitting. What constitutes right and fitting usually involves the view of some personal authority figure of theirs.

Clues to anger in 5/6/7s is a certain righteous quality in voice and manner. They know how and what things should be and tell others so. They also may quietly, correctly, patiently, explain things to listeners. Sometimes the cooler and more detached they sound and the more carefully they elucidate details of situations the angrier they are. Detachment is always a sign of emotional distance, and frequently that distance will be from feelings of anger and the fear that such anger raises in them.

Director/Directee Relationships

Directors would do well to avoid restatement of what their 5/6/7 directees say. Even moreso they need to stay away from interpretation and analysis. People in this space are sensitive to having words put into their mouths, sometimes because they have carefully thought out their own statement and sometimes because they have spent much of their lives being spoken for.

It is hard many times for 5/6/7 directees to ask for anything in direction: time, attention, concern. They often were children who could be put aside in crises, who naturally step back for other more assertive and demanding family members. Now, as adults, they may know that things are different, but old habits persist. Even with the more outgoing 6s and 7s, and surely with 5s, it is well to indicate verbally or nonverbally one's availability and willingness to focus on them and their lives.

> I know you really mean it when you say you have time for me. But I still find myself hurrying to say what I want to say, even feeling a little guilty after we've met, especially if we're at all over our time. It not only doesn't seem quite right to have you give me all this attention, it seems strange, too. I don't usually find myself in this sort of position.

While the people they care about remain important— and loyalty is a priority for them—5/6/7s need to be reminded to tend and foster relationships with people. Doing so involves not only words and actions showing care for others, it also means revealing themselves to their companions in life. One way to become more self-revelatory is to use "I" statements. This simple and tried communication skill makes for conscious, deliberate behavior that furthers interdependent involvement with others.

One of the confusing aspects of relationships for 5/6/7s is around the issue of safety and gradual trust-building. When is it important to respect 5/6/7s privacy needs? When does examination of the fruitfulness of their detachment and withdrawal need to become a challenge? People in this space often need to buy time before they respond. One way they do so is by saying the equivalent of "Let me think about it." Often they genuinely need to do so, but sometimes it is a way to withhold self-revelation. Distinguishing which is the case becomes one of the issues in direction.

When 5/6/7s expose what they feel about something it is like taking a stand. Actually doing that, coming down on one side of an issue, is to run the risk that they may be wrong, that they will look foolish, that the director will not have confidence in them. Fantasizing the consequences of various choices can make these options more concrete and real. It can even touch them into feelings that rise up as they imagine possibilities.

As directors, it is important to encourage their own decision, precisely because it is their own. Asking them what it is they genuinely want in a particular instance can be a form of reassurance. It states that the director is not here to give out opinions. It is all right, it is mature and therefore preferable, to take their eyes off the director as expert. Any way to gently underline this dynamic can move 5/6/7s to trust in their own authority. Communicating comfort with the fact that each decision need not be a perfect one can also free 5/6/7s in decision-making.

After invoking 5/6/7s' own authority, directors, as said before, need to let them think and talk around options until they become comfortable with decisions. There is a trap here, however, which directors need to be aware of: 5/6/7s often extend conversations to find out what the director is thinking in an effort to discover what they should think. This is especially true if they consider the director an expert, which a director often is seen to be. A focus on helping them test their courage in small ways can move them away from the director and onto their own responses.

Life is a series of steps rather than leaps, of moving along day to day with some consistency rather than freezing in paralysis and then rushing to catch up. Addressing life little by little can afford a kinesthetic reference point for 5/6/7s around the feel of the flow of their lives. From back and forth, stop and start, they come to experience bodily a more steady movement of small, consistent steps.

Looking to the director for the right way to live can have its positive side as well. Oftentimes 5/6/7s are reluctant to do things, to take on projects, assignments, and tasks, because these seem too formidable. They may even feel a lack of ability to perform them. The courage to try can come by highlighting for 5/6/7s that someone they trust sees them as capable. This encouragement may be enough to lead them to risk what seems frighteningly unknown and unsure.

It is important to confirm 5/6/7s' thoughts and insights at appropriate moments. This not only helps them to trust in themselves, but in interaction as a way to wisdom. The process of exchanging ideas and observations, of feelings and insights, leads not only to vulnerability but to growth. Such exchange deepens and broadens awareness and fosters a contemplative openness and letting go. Confirmation differs from affirmation. It is a validation of their own assessment as being one shared by others, and it gives them confidence in their knowledge.

Finally, there is always need for directors of 5/6/7s to attend to the compulsion around collecting more and more data. People in this dynamic need to put limits on research, to experience how much information and knowledge is enough. Sometimes it is valuable to ask that very question: "How much feels like enough to you?"

To ask this moves considerations to a level of personal experience and away from scanning options. What does enough feel like? When am I finished looking and observing? Which of the options I am considering touch me at an affective level, or, to put it another way, which ones do I really want in some personal way? What possibilities hold energy is another expression of the same thing, since energy and emotion always exist together. This reminder is important for 5/6/7s.

However it is done, somehow highlighting with 5/6/7 directees which of their possibilities are viable, real, and life-giving is the intent. Helping them touch into their feelings will move them eventually out of the stance of mere observers and into the stream of their lives. Choice is around little things. Making these small decisions, 5/6/7s learn, is not so frightening. Helping with that learning is one of the contributions directors for people in this basic stance can make.

CHAPTER 7

The 5 Directee

It may be well to begin a discussion of 5 directees by saying that, contrary to many of the descriptions one may read about this space, 5s are not necessarily intellectual or bookish.

Rather, they are focused on their perceptions, collect data, and gather information. They are always looking for the key that will unlock meaning; they somehow believe, or at least hope, that there is some construct or inner map that will order what often seems to be chaotic reality.

They are very fearful about upsetting the inner order or system they have made to remove this chaos. If it is challenged by new information they feel lost and grow defensive until they can test whether this data is right, whether they can resonate with it. Once they synthesize new input with existing knowledge they feel confident again. Their paralysis melts; they return to a sense of safety.

Directors of 5s need to remember this dynamic, especially as directees move to deeper levels. What may appear to be resistance may indeed be so, but it comes from this instinctive process. Their 5 directees may need time to themselves to self-connect and integrate what is new.

When 5s feel lost, they know from experience that they are vulnerable to being taken advantage of. Until they can again emerge with what is right and ordered they are gullible and, at least in their own eyes, look foolish. It is important for them to find a direction relationship which is safe, where they won't be pushed around, hurried, spoken for, interrupted, and treated as insignificant. These and other disrespectful responses make them feel victimized.

Their life experience has taught 5s to be self-sufficient in order to avoid situations where they will be taken advantage of. They hesitate to ask for what they need in the form of attention, time, and presence; they prefer to satisfy their own concrete, physical needs as well. It may be more important in this space than in any other for directors to pay attention to health issues, sleep patterns, diet, and digestion. These often give clues to what is going on with a person, as well as signaling physical problems. Fives will often fail to note signals of disease, pain, and physical impairment and need to be reminded to do so.

Of course, it is important to distinguish with 5s whether their desire to take things away and work on them alone is a healthy or compulsive response to their instinctive perceptual approach to reality. Merely asking the question may be sufficient to resolve issues of compulsive withdrawal, but this is not always the case. Perhaps it is here that 5s are helped by being asked to relate this impulse to remove themselves with similar situations in their past. Touching 5s into their affective history, particularly their fears and sufferings, often opens them to their own answers, keeping the director's intervention minimal.

When they can ask their own questions of themselves and respond to them from their own life story, 5s retain an important sense of self-mastery and maturity. They learn to honor their past rather than forget it and come to realize what the events of their lives have done to them.

Fives often get much perceptual mileage out of small bits of their experience; what may seem to directors as very little information can yield a wealth of insight for them. The compulsion to relate abstemiously to life manifests itself not only in stinginess regarding material things but also shows up in their perceptual world. Life seems, many times, to be lean and poor for those 5s who are devoid of richness of feeling and insight.

Directors from the other basic spaces on the enneagram sometimes find this a problem in directing 5s. For 8/9/1 directors, 5s may offer a challenge to stay attentive and engaged. Boredom and sleepiness may make keeping focus difficult during their sessions with 5s. For 2/3/4s, the temptation to pump energy into a session by filling silences, questioning excessively, and putting words into directees' mouths, can result in minimizing rather than increasing exchange.

> Direction is a real problem for me. I honestly don't know what to say when I'm there. Either things are worked out already and there's no need to go back over them, or else they're so mixed up I couldn't put words on them if I tried. Sometimes I honestly wonder what the point of my going for spiritual direction is.

If 5 directees actually do begin to process during their direction sessions, they can become so busy looking at their lives that observing them becomes the only reality. They can be so taken up in wanting to see what is going on that they forget to bring directors along with them. Once something has been clarified and has become experiential rather than theoretical, it is obvious to them. Therefore, it must be obvious to their directors, too. Surely their directors see what they see.

"Seeing" reality is probably more important in this space than in any other. Because it is the emphasis, hearing may be downplayed, even forgotten about. Five directees may completely miss what directors suggest or question, so involved are they in what, of course, must be so and recognized as such by anyone observing with them.

Encouraging them to expand terse and cryptic remarks can help them move to the realm of the auditory, so that they begin to hear themselves and their directors. This exchange enlarges merely organizing and fitting their own perceptions together. When they do speak their ideas aloud, they may sound overly objective. Pointing out this detached quality of speech may afford them helpful behavioral data about their attitude to their reality.

Directors who ask for information may sometimes feel they are asking 5s to reiterate what seems obvious to them. It is important for directors to remember that their encouragement of 5 directees to put words on their experience serves an important purpose, that of connecting them with the outer world and offering them the benefits of expression and relationship. Another person's perception may well enrich one's own. Another person may look at 5s' life history with the kind of respect and dignified sensitivity that encourages them to honor and respect themselves.

The direction relationship may become an analogy for 5s of other life relationships. They discover that there are people who care to listen and understand, who may have contributions to make to 5s' understanding of themselves. When the atmosphere is a safe one, one where they do not feel pushed around and where they are called to some sort of accountability and personal sharing, life is less dry. It is deepened by levels of enriched affective experience. People can enter 5s' inner world when the paralysis of fear melts and they open its door. Life no longer passes them by; it is something even more worthwhile because it is shared by another.

Probably at no other place on the enneagram is it more important to gently invite response from directees. To do so necessitates on the part of directors an appraisal, whether consciously or intuitively made, of readiness on the part of their 5 directees. When the time is right, directors of 5s may be amazed at the overflow of communication that comes from them. When it does come, it must be carefully listened to, even if it seems prolonged. It is important to 5 directees, and so it must be important to their directors.

> I never really thought anybody was interested in what went on inside me. Then I began to see Ann for direction. I think it was her eyes, the way she looked at me, with so much respect and care and attention. I learned somebody else could see what I see and spend time with what I wanted to spend time with. I was valuable to somebody, finally, after all these years.

CHAPTER 8

The 6 Directee

The energy of 6s is a back and forth one. Their characteristic ambivalence comes from seeing so many options
and finding it hard to select among them. Some say that
they are the most difficult of enneagram spaces to predict;
it is hard to know what response will be forthcoming in
any given situation. Will they move out or will they
withdraw? One can never be sure.

Sixes often project their ambivalence onto others, who
they accuse of being unable to make up their minds. For
directors it is important to distinguish between their expression of an inability to make decisions and a determination not to. When 6s say, "I can't," they may, in reality, be
saying, "I won't." The "I won't" often comes from a fear
of venturing out beyond the safety of considerations to the
risk of commitment and action.

The duty to obey is a strong motivation for 6s when they
do move into action. When this duty is merely that, a
feeling that they must do what authority says, it results in
a tentative, shaky, halfhearted doing. When it flows from
the affective level of commitment, 6s can be calm and
strong in the face of whatever opposition lies in their path.

A major task, therefore, for directors of 6s is to plumb
with them the depth of their feelings around the movements and choices in their lives. What will make an option
emerge from the many as the right and fitting one depends
on both the emotional and kinesthetic feel of it. If this
discernment is not done, 6s move from a cautious, shaky
stance, which often shows in their voice, body, and speech

style, to the flip side of that—over-sure, dogmatic, some-times patronizing words and behavior. This back and forth from uncertainty to sureness signals that 6s are into hyperperception, spinning on in their mental function with option after option, possibility after possibility. It is important for directors to weigh the quality of the decisions 6s announce to them. If that quality is quiet and calm, the decision comes from the place of inner authority. If it is not, it may indicate something that was determined because 6s found themselves in a dangerous spot. It may result from their picking up what directors as authority figures deem the thing to do. Whatever may have motivated the decision, if it feels off center to the director as observer, it will probably contribute to further am-bivalence and procrastination in the 6 directee. What looked to the director like a firm decision may well prove not to be; their 6 directees will return for another round of accelerating and then applying brakes, as Riso has put it.

> I was absolutely sure we had laid to rest the issue about how to relate to the boss at our previous session. Frank sounded so definite and confident about what he was going to say and do. Then there we were back at the old, scared place with nothing done. He was quaking like a little kid all over again. In retrospect, I realized that it was I who had thought we'd settled on a plan of action, not Frank. He'd just caught my en-thusiasm, but it really wasn't coming from him. He thought I wanted it, so he tried to want it, too.

There is an inviting, even seductive quality in 6s. They tend to be playful and teasing and have a whimsical humor that engages others. The child in them expresses itself in a guileless and open manner. Their perception of themselves as innocent, as fearful of being ganged up on and harmed, highlights how unprotected they feel when they risk moving out into the environment and interacting with people. As Palmer has said, 6s identify with the underdog, unlike 8s who see themselves as helping the underdog to find justice (Palmer 1988). Sixes see themselves as the people who need to receive help.

The other side of this appealing and endearing manner, which often expresses itself in a smile, is one of caution, suspicion, and, in more extreme cases, paranoia. It is important when dealing with 6s, both in their personal relationships and in the dynamics of direction, to help them distinguish between accurate perceptions and projections that rise out of their own feelings of not being safe.

Sixes can be critical of others, righteous in accusations, angry at being disillusioned by authority figures they trusted, including their directors. They can also be angry at not having others respect them when they are in the position of an authority figure. This anger is not so much because they consider themselves important as it is that they value respect for authority no matter who holds it. They are not really so afraid of danger, according to Palmer, as they are of authority and what it can do to them. Actually, they come to see, as they become more converted, that they have handed over power to authority figures, and they fear the consequences of having done so.

Directors, then, need to assure 6s that they are walking with them on the path to decision and action which forms the challenge of conversion in this space. When they feel cornered, when their loyalty and duty have resulted in their having allowed themselves to be taken advantage of, directors need to allow that anger over having too much to do. The director's role is to help 6s realize what this anger is telling them. When 6s are sad and brooding because they failed to act out of confusion and powerlessness, directors need to be there to assist them to accept themselves.

Discouragement needs to be watched for in 6s because it may not be openly expressed and can lead to withdrawal and self-deprecating behaviors. Sixes hate their helplessness but feel inadequate to do anything about it, at least by themselves. Encouraging them to participate in support groups can prove helpful. Possibly it is 5s and 6s who most benefit from group situations where they learn to articulate their experience and find support and assistance.

When accepted by directors and by themselves, 6s discover that a compulsive leap into action may not be the best of responses. Rather, moving to the level of self-understanding can bring them to where they can know what, if any, response is the right one. Puns are of help for 6s in arriving at insight about themselves and their experience. Dreams in which puns occur can provide the perspective of humor 6s need to take themselves less seriously.

> I dreamed about the Brothers Grimm last night. They were writing stories about my life with chapter after chapter of events and I was reading them aloud while they wrote. My voice got deeper and deeper until I couldn't hear it anymore. Then somebody said in my ear: "You're one of them. You're a Grimm brother, too." When I woke up I thought, yeah, you can say that again!

Sixes can, indeed, become grim and merciless toward themselves and others, especially when the law becomes larger than life. One compulsion for 6s is to hold whatever authority person embodies the right as overly important in their lives. This law of right and order becomes the center of existence. Everyone, including themselves, is seen as living around it and out of it. If they are not keeping the law they are breaking or bending it because it is more fitting to do that. The law is never out of their consideration.

Holding up this dynamic and asking 6s to note whether it is exaggerated or not can help them to place rules, regulations, order, and rightness into a perspective that frees rather than binds and inhibits them. The oppression of living in a dutiful and right manner is one reason 6s can become almost nonfunctional. Whatever directors can do to assist 6s to notice how their fear can accelerate to irrational proportions contributes to their growth. They are enabled by such insight to move into the gradual flow of their lives beyond the fits and starts they can compulsively get caught into.

Directors need to become part of what their 6 directees perceive as a safe refuge. This does not mean that they are there to protect their directees from harm, but rather to create an atmosphere in which 6s can lay down their defensive armor and move freely among considerations to decisions without the danger of criticism.

The authority 6s are inclined to give over to their directors can be used by directors to encourage 6s to move to their own authority. Once in touch with interior authority they are at the level of feeling. This inner confidence can be trusted. Sixes can invoke it in choosing among the myriad of options, many of which they create to keep themselves inactive and therefore safe. Freedom and initiative replace procrastination as 6s move toward conversion in companionship with a director who encourages them to trust themselves.

CHAPTER 9

The 7 Directee

One misconception other people have about 7s is that they are always happy. They are not, but they would like to change life into a more pleasant and pleasurable place. They like to dream of possibilities and imagine the best. They are also outgoing and friendly, though this social response often covers a deep fear. When one has ventured out from safety, such a great value for 7s, one feels unprotected.

If anything, the fear of the 7 approaches the level of terror. While this terror has something to do with aloneness and vulnerability, it also refers to an intensity 7s feel around the chaos threatening all the 5/6/7s. Sensory stimulation is so strong at the 7 space that reality takes on exaggerated proportions. Perception is the way of life for 5/6/7s; at the 7 place, where it especially bombards with impressions, it can feel overwhelming. Their experience of sensory overstimulation is similar to the enlargement of problems and fears that happens when people lie awake at night. No wonder, then, that 7s want to turn darkness into light.

With these awarenesses as background, it becomes obvious that 7s need to find a particularly safe environment in direction. Since they inevitably venture out, they become very frightened. They need directors who understand how 7s look at life and who will be with them in their efforts to create a place without harm. When they find such directors 7s are more able to admit to themselves the extent of their chaotic feeling and let its reality touch them.

If directors accept them at face value as a jolly, happy lot, 7s will oblige by playing with the plans, patterns, and systems with which they amuse themselves. If, however, directors can cut through the lightheartedness, they will facilitate their 7 directees' admitting how dark, lonely, and unpleasant they fear the world really is. They suspect there is not meaning to it all; but if they act as though there were, they may be able to hold reality together. Their philosophy, whether they express it in word or action, holds that everything is for the best. This is their brave effort to master life.

> I've fixed up my new house and it's a very cozy and inviting place, someplace I want to be able to come home to and settle in. I have all sorts of plans about how I'm going to entertain there. But, you know what? I'm never home. I just can't stay there for some reason. I go out for dinner with friends and we sit around until we've solved all the problems of the world. That's when I feel most comfortable.

Sevens captivate directors with their extensive information and the wealth of insight they have in many areas, including spiritual direction. Sometimes they sound not only informed but in touch, so articulately can they speak about problems and concerns in their lives. As 2/3/4s fill in silences to stay connected, 7s may keep up a conversation to fend off terror. Often they are unaware that this is what they are doing, so distant are they from their fear. As the conversion process deepens for them and these fears rise to the surface, directors need gently to quiet 7s' efforts to cover the fear they can no longer deny with a blanket of verbiage about ideas, plans, and possibilities.

This is not always an easy thing to do. Their ideas are interesting to directors in their own part of the enneagram. Those elsewhere often find it either stimulating to listen to their stories and jokes, or fun to play the child role with them. These temptations to sit back and enjoy 7s can work against them in direction. It serves no purpose, however, to press them firmly to their darkness and pain. Rather, to remind them of and touch them briefly and lightly to threatening reality again and again helps them become accustomed to it.

Directors of 7s often find them focused on the theme of fidelity in relationships. Sevens become filled with enthusiasm over anything new. They have a child's urgency to have whatever they want, whether food, enjoyment, or response. It can even be as simple as the impulse to throw out planned agendas or activities for something they now deem more important.

It is hard for 7s to postpone gratification. When this dynamic applies to other human beings, it can lead them to an "out of sight out of mind" mentality; when someone new comes along they are often captivated and want to involve themselves with that person, even when this contradicts a previous commitment to someone else. Because sensory stimulation has a high priority for 7s, sexual expression often figures into the issue.

Sevens are curious and friendly. They also can have tantrum-like outbursts of temper, which are sudden and passionate and can surprise directors. Like 6s, who have similar bursts of temper, they may feel cornered and hemmed in, either by choices they have made or the frustration of their desires. Such aggression often signals the panic they feel over fear of having to endure pain and deprivation. It is usually short-lived, and once expressed allows them to move on to other concerns.

Another kind of anger is more quiet. It is expressed in bluntness, in intellectual barbs, and a good-natured sort of quizzing. This kind of anger serves the purpose for 7s of finding out what people think, where they are on a subject, and how to fit their ideas and them into already existing schemes. Its intent is a social one, and its base is in that fear of chaos which motivates much of the 7's behavior.

He was always making biting little remarks and then watching for how I took what he said. It was like a game or contest but it had an edge to it, sort of like he was smiling shyly from behind the door while he tossed out hand grenades. At first I didn't know quite what to do with the whole thing, but I eventually learned it was a way for him to be in contact with me. Once I figured that out we talked about it and the situation got more comfortable.

The source of the 7's fear is that he or she may not be "on top" perceptually. Not to know, not to have order, not to possess the most information on a subject possible means to be out of control. Perhaps, 7s fear, they may fall into that always-threatening disorder.

Suggesting that they stay in the present rather than pick up and put down future possibility after future possibility, interesting plan after interesting plan, helps 7s learn that the present does not necessarily mean deprivation. There is life here and now, and there will continue to be life enough in the future. Whatever is here is sufficient to survive darkness and emptiness. Reality here and now contains emotional passion and, therefore, genuine energy.

Sevens need the challenge to let their feelings be experienced. Although they may look and sound warmly engaged, there is a distance and withdrawal at this as at the other spaces in this triad. Their first instinct is to withdraw, but they fight its indication of fear and bravely move out to engage the environment and people in it. Directors who are not aware of this tendency toward emotional detachment from personal reality and from the direction relationship may wonder why so little progress occurs in direction. The reason is often that the issues and insights 7s speak about with such enthusiasm remain on a merely perceptual rather than heartfelt level.

Self-protection and urgency that their needs be satisfied allows 7s in compulsion to be deviant and detached even as they retain an aura of innocence and childlikeness. It is only when they move from disproportionate attention around fulfilling their wants that 7s grow into a genuine care for others. Like the children they often resemble, 7s in conversion learn by living that love demands postponement, pain, and sacrifice; it is not always pleasant. This realization can be nearly overwhelming. To have a director to share it with provides the courage not to run away.

CHAPTER 10

The 5/6/7 Director

The same characteristics that affect 5/6/7s as directees are present, of course, when they function as directors. Like people in all spaces, 5/6/7s desire to offer others what they themselves want to have in the direction relationship. Like everyone else, they come to learn that what helps them is not always what helps directees from other stances. People differ so much that the very things that are most valuable to one enneagram space may militate against movement and growth for those in another. We now turn to how this reality applies when 5/6/7s function as spiritual directors.

Objectivity vs. *Detachment*

The gift of 5/6/7 directors, as well as their weakness, lies in their tendency to approach life perceptually. Directees of people in this part of the enneagram sometimes feel they are objects being examined rather than people being companioned. In an effort to leave directees free, 5/6/7 directors are inclined to stay too far away from them; they instinctively observe rather than interact. In order to respect their directees' privacy, 5/6/7 directors may remain uninvolved; they may fail to challenge and relate sufficiently to those they direct.

Above all, 5/6/7s value being listened to by other people. They are appreciative of respect for their ideas and life experience. Such respect is something they often feel has been dealt out in small measure to them in their lifetime. They want to offer this opportunity for time, attention, and space to think and speak and act to their directees. Sometimes what they intend as a sign of respect is experienced by directees as an expression of detachment and disinterest.

One reason 5/6/7 directors seem distant is that they frequently relate around the ideas, issues, and data of experience rather than to persons. Directees can feel that their personal struggles and emotions are secondary to the more objective information with which their 5/6/7 directors concern themselves. As data is gathered, 5/6/7 directors tend to categorize it according to some inner order or pattern. Directees may feel that they are categorized along with what they have expressed.

When directees feel themselves considered as objects for study, they react to what they sometimes call boxing and labeling in various ways. For 8/9/1s this often occasions anger and frustration over not being recognized in their totality. For 2/3/4s it provides opportunity for anxiety; they wonder what their 5/6/7 directors are thinking as they silently listen and evaluate. No matter what space directees come from they may be inclined in such a situation to sift out the affective components from their communications to 5/6/7 directors. They tend to present their directors with what seems to be wanted: objective information.

> I finally gave up on my director. I felt she was gathering my entire life history for a case study on me rather than really being with me. It was as though she had to find some cause and work to a solution. I decided to look for somebody who wouldn't make me feel I was under a microscope while she jotted notes on what she saw there.

The Value of Objectivity

The gift of perceptual emphasis so instinctive for 5/6/7 directors expresses itself in careful attention. For this focus to be of help to directees, it needs to be joined with genuine emotion. As enlightened directors, 5/6/7s listen with the care they want others to offer them. They attend to both the verbal and nonverbal communication of their directees. They pick up sensory clues, especially visual ones. If they can remember to share these observations with their directees, they can often move them to deeper levels of feeling. Helping directees be aware of their expression, posture, and behavior assists their self-understanding.

Much of what 5/6/7 directors see can offer insights about their directees' interior lives. As directors, it is important for them to share those insights, even when these are still at the level of hunches and intuitions. Although not always substantiated by data, such communications are valuable and should not be withheld. They will tend to withhold these, however, because they are accustomed to expressing only what has been worked out in their own inner world.

Reluctance to share unprocessed reality can have negative ramifications for 5/6/7 directors. One of these effects of withholding information until it is fully processed is that it may lead directees to lose the focus on their own experience. Instead, their directees may find themselves taken up with trying to figure out what is going on with their directors.

It is important that 5/6/7 directors remind themselves to let their directees know what they are seeing and where their thought processes are taking them. Articulating hypotheses they hold as well as insights they have come to in an effort to understand joins 5/6/7 directors with their directees.

When 5/6/7 directors model putting out their own unfinished reality, their directees will be more able to do so. Once 5/6/7 directors suspend judgments of rightness or wrongness on their listening and understanding, they can assist directees to do the same.

> I feel sure my directees are interested in getting out
> all the information around an issue, so I tend to wait
> until they seem to have done so. What I've learned
> over the years is that they would often like to know
> how I'm feeling or what's going on in my head about
> what they're saying. When I pick up that that's the
> case I've learned to switch gears from taking in the
> content of what they're saying and let them in on
> what's going on with me. Sometimes I think the
> information about their experience is of more interest
> to me than to them.

In fact, gathering information in order to come to conclusion and resolution may, indeed, be a greater concern for 5/6/7 directors than for their directees. Life is not a problem to be enlightened or solved, converted 5/6/7s learn. It is a mystery to be lived, to be entered into and walked around and known more fully. The more contemplative 5/6/7 directors become, the more they know this to be so. When they respond out of this learning they can be effective directors, providing help from their observing and objective gift.

The Emphasis on Data

We now consider further some of the positive and negative ramifications of 5/6/7 directors' strong perceptual instinct. What happens in direction relationships when 5/6/7 directors are taken with the information presented to them? What happens when they focus on this information as a primary avenue for growth and change, insight and conversion, awareness and contemplation for their directees?

Directors in the 5/6/7 part of the enneagram spend conscientious efforts gathering and understanding the content of what their directees say. They instinctively connect and interrelate various aspects of these communications, often finding order in what directees experience as confusion or chaotic bits of reality. Because they are outside looking in, 5/6/7 directors have more perspective and objectivity and can see patterns, causes and effects, and connections in what directees may regard as the disorganized mess of their reality.

Since 5/6/7s carefully assess what directees communicate, they may find it hard to move with other ideas than their own, especially if directees cannot clearly substantiate why they see their reality differently. It may be hard for 5/6/7 directors to accept opinions and assessments from directees when these differ from their own. As directees speak, images and symbols may come to 5/6/7 directors' minds which differ from those their directees put forth. In the presence of this perceptual dissonance, they may deny, or at least question their directees' reality. They may try to fit it into the framework they carry inside themselves rather than adjust that framework based on directees' response to it.

In fact, 5/6/7 directors may well have clearer and more accurate perceptions than their directees do. Nevertheless, they need to remember that their directees' denial of or inability to understand the assessments they offer them are part of the information present in the direction relationship. As such, it becomes part of the reality to be known and worked with.

Not only do 5/6/7 directors need to let go of those compulsions that urge them to push for the right information, so, too, do directors in other spaces need to let go of whatever it is they exaggerate to compulsion. Directors who are 2/3/4s need to refrain from moving directees along to doing something before they have even experienced their reality. Those who are 8/9/1s need to let directees join their affective experience with characteristic activity or perceptual emphases rather than hold them forcibly in the realm of feeling.

It is characteristic of people in each triad to assume that life is the way they see it and that when clarity of communication happens all people will view life the same way. Such will never be the case. Part of human limitation means that, try as we may, we will filter our awarenesses through our unique and partial consciousness.

Given enneagram descriptions of the triads, it seems to be most difficult to understand the world view of people behind us on the enneagram circle. Thus 2/3/4s, who are least in touch with their feelings, find 8/9/1s, who instinctively meet life from this feeling function, hard to understand. For 5/6/7s it is the 2/3/4 triad that provides the greatest challenge, since 5/6/7s are furthest away from the doing/behavioral response with which 2/3/4s meet life. 8/9/1s find 5/6/7s something of an enigma because perception is both the deepest hidden function for 8/9/1s and the instinct of 5/6/7s. In other words, looking over our shoulder at the preceding triad and accurately seeing it is not easy to do. It often results in mistranslation of behavior and misunderstanding of experience.

While the triad behind one's own remains something of a mystery, the one ahead is less so. This is because the auxiliary function in each triad is the instinctive one in the triad ahead. Therefore, 2/3/4s, whose perceptual function is their helping/auxiliary one, are likely to understand the perceptual 5/6/7s. 5/6/7s, helped by their feelings, resonate with 8/9/1s, the instinctively feeling persons. 8/9/1s, who invoke doing/behavior with some ease, can relate to 2/3/4s in their instinctive reality.

While these generalizations can prove helpful in relationships, it is important to remember that they are just that: generalizations. It is the depth of the journey of living which best enables people to understand self and one another, as has been said before. Nevertheless, given that unity at the center of human struggle, genuine knowing through shared experience would seem most easily to take place along the lines described.

All directors need to open themselves beyond the narrow world of their own instinct out of which their particular kind of compulsions are formed. All directors need to be watchful for the kind of insensitivity that urgently propels them to characteristic reactions. The more they lack a contemplative attitude, the more they are blinded by such compulsion, and the less able they are to allow the reality of their directees' lives.

Problems of the Perceptual Approach

The tendency to gather information about life, to take it in perceptually, manifests itself in 5/6/7 directors' focus on the exact content of the words their directees speak. Asking people to define words exactly, to provide data for things they have stated, to think carefully so that their response matches their experience accurately are all examples of this concern for the factual and precise.

Calling directees to this careful statement can be helpful. It encourages 8/9/1s to look for patterns they might otherwise not pay attention to. It provides them with a reason to step away from their intense emotion to where they can see situations as separate from themselves. When it holds them too rigidly to such considerations, however, it can result in their rebelling and resisting efforts. When properly applied, these approaches can help them broaden to include their perceptual function in the conversion process.

While 2/3/4s may find help as well through applying a more perceptual emphasis on their experience, encouragement to do so may communicate that who they are is not acceptable. Attempts to shape their response, to urge it into channels where 2/3/4 directees are not inclined to go, may freeze them inside so that self-awareness becomes impossible. They may very well go on apparently relating, which they are inclined to do, but only on the outside.

Literal 5/6/7 directors will go on picking up what their 2/3/4 directees may see as continued communication. In reality, these factual directors also pick up distance and lack of feeling. If 5/6/7 directors point out this superficial quality to them, their 2/3/4 directees will probably only freeze the more, even as they experience an increased desire to give their directors what they seem to be asking for.

The cycle continues with 2/3/4 directees feeling less and less adequate as they strive to figure out what it is their 5/6/7 directors think they lack and how to supply it. It matters not for these directors to say they only want data, information that is fitting and resonant with reality and consistent. When they hear their directors ask for something they are not giving, 2/3/4s feel they have failed to be the right kind of directees.

Since 5/6/7 directors take in so much data, they are sometimes ahead of directees who do not possess this same instinct. What they observe as directors, 5/6/7s assume their directees must also observe. Actually, they may have moved ahead of their directees, at least perceptually. It is important for 5/6/7s in the direction situation to remind themselves of this dynamic and pause now and then to ask whether they need to take their directees along with them to wherever their own perceptions have led.

One way to do that is by sharing their own process of making associations and integrating the experience directees present to them. Communicating what they see and what it says to them forces 5/6/7 directors to slow down to the perceptual pace of their directees.

> I've noticed you've used the words puzzle and maze a few times now. That brings to mind for me a picture of you searching around for something you haven't arrived at yet and I'm wondering what it is you might be looking for. I thought I'd tell you what I'm thinking in case it might be a helpful question for you, too.

Beyond Perception

Another way to be where their directees are is to attend consciously to the other functions of feeling and doing.

Reminding themselves of the emotional component of what they are presented with, as well as how receiving it affects them, broadens out 5/6/7s' awareness to another aspect of reality. Thus, the possibility of getting caught up in the urgency of compulsive perceiving is lessened. Considering what decisions and actions might flow from the data may also enhance the reality presented and engage them in ways beyond merely taking in data.

To whomever they are offered, 5/6/7 directors' bald statements of what they see as real can put off and disturb directees. This is especially true, of course, when directees are in a vulnerable or fragile place in their journey. The tendency of 5/6/7s to theorize and generalize, to look with too much focus on long-term continuity and patterned reality, can result in mere verbal exchanges about experience. The goal in direction, they may need to remind themselves, is to provide an atmosphere which facilitates directees' movement in their own lives.

The contribution of 5/6/7 directors lies, as it does for all directors, in this same instinct from which their compulsions take shape. Their observation of trends and patterns and of rhythms and themes, as well as their natural propensity for linking ideas together can prove to be the most helpful dynamics they bring to their sessions. Where life seems formless to a directee, 5/6/7 directors often struggle to see it otherwise and in the process help their directees to do so as well. While 5/6/7 directors can at times question too intently in an effort to get to the essence of their directees' experience, they can also ask the vital and penetrating question that opens up a way to go or makes things fall into place.

When 5/6/7s hold the total persons of their directees in mind rather than merely these persons' words about themselves, direction moves from the level of ideas to genuine human exchange. When they assist directees to acknowledge and own their own reality rather than accept insights and information as substitutes for it, they actually meet them. What had been exchanging observations becomes relationship.

Directors in the 5/6/7 stance grow in their own ability to be loyal and committed as their own journey progresses. Their fidelity and confidentiality can be relied on. They also are able to hold onto information previously communicated which applies in current situations. Often they are surprised at how significant this ability can be to directees. After all, they are only being present and sharing what they observed. And yet, that quiet and supportive encouragement to explore and ask about one's reality may be the element missing in a directee's process.

> I know as a director I tend to be rather unobtrusive. I don't do a lot, really. I'm surprised when I get the feedback—which I often seem to—that people find a question I asked opened up everything for them. From my side, I was just trying to understand what they were saying. That seems to be what they also need to do and my asking helps them ask.

The Place of Wisdom

It takes time for trust to grow for 5/6/7s. This holds true whether they are directors or directees. As directees, 5/6/7s only open themselves in relationship when they have tested the reality of their directors' concern manifested in their being taken seriously. As directors, they commit themselves to the direction relationship and the person of their individual directees only when their careful concern for these directees' experience is respected and appreciated. When they have ascertained that such is the case, they no longer hold in their ideas and insights but flow into a communication of their own process which often facilitates that of their directees.

From being quiet and somewhat distant observers, they move to become willing, helpful resource persons. They do their homework around direction sessions conscientiously and enthusiastically the more comfortable they feel with a directee. While this looking into and preparing and evaluating and trying to understand is never quite enough from their vantage point, it is a rich contribution to the process of their directees. In their relentless search for more information leading to deeper insight, they can sometimes make the one remark or speak the significant phrase or name the relevant hypothesis crucial to their directees' movement.

Because they intend to be competent and understanding, 5/6/7 directors may become hyperperceptive rather than wise. If they find compassion and care for their directees, if they take in their pain and joy and sadness and anxiety as well as their thoughts and perceptual connections, they prepare their directees to open up their hearts. Then, in the safety of growing trust, the directors will offer response rather than withhold intuitions. They will share relevant experiences of their own and tell their directees how they feel not only about what these directees tell them but about their own personal reality as well.

Knowledge that thus comes to rest in their hearts, that becomes experience, makes them wise directors. All of this is made possible for 5/6/7 directors, as for others, because of the depth with which they come to know their own lack and limitation, their own gift and contribution. They are always looking to know more, to be wise, to be understanding. Directors in the 5/6/7 stance find that, at their best, that is truly what they offer their directees.

> I care about the people I direct. I take time with them to listen. I write down what happens in sessions. I study over my notes and ask the questions of their input that I'd ask about my own, were I in their place. That's the respect I like to have and it's what I want to give others.

The 8/9/1 Triad

CHAPTER 11

Directees Who Are 8/9/1s

Now we turn to people in this final triad, observing their instinctive response to reality. We attempt to look out at life from their unique stance. Again, we highlight general themes and issues for all three numbers. We then move on to each in turn. Finally, we use these observations to address directors who come from these spaces with the purpose of highlighting the communication issues that can arise as this space encounters the others on the way to conversion.

Effects of an Exaggerated Feeling Center

Whatever function is most instinctive for each of us becomes operative before awareness, let alone decision and choice. We react without consciousness from our activity, perceptual, or feeling function. Only when we know our instinctive response and observe its reality can we unmask instincts grown to compulsion. Such unmasking takes away the power of the compulsion and leads to more and more freedom of choice. Now we see how the instinctive feeling function affects the spiritual journeys, the lives, of people in the 8/9/1 triad.

For 8/9/1s feeling is present even before they are aware of it. Perhaps it would be more accurate to say that the feeling function becomes the focus for 8/9/1s, sometimes because they struggle to control or properly express this feeling, sometimes because they determine it must be eliminated or submerged until it no longer is an issue. These latter 8/9/1s may even deny that they have anger or other emotions, so successfully have they driven them into their shadow. Life continues to focus around the feeling function nevertheless. Whether they bury, deny, or control it, feeling is the primary instinct.

The basic reaction for 8/9/1s is that of liking or not liking. They trust this sense because, as they say, it comes from their gut. Another way to speak about this basic reaction is that it is body based. When the response is one of liking something or someone, it or the person is judged as good. Such judgment of goodness is usually connected with what is pleasurable. When the response is of disliking something or someone, it or the person carries either a sense of badness, or of causing pain, or of disturbing what is settled.

One of the accompanying dynamics around an exaggerated feeling function is that of being stuck emotionally in the past. Undigested life experiences from 8/9/1s' personal history influence present reactions. Another way to say this is that they meet the present with their past, and often a past that has been parked and forgotten so that it remains unexperienced. 8/9/1s tend to feel so intensely that they hold off the full import of their life history when it happens. Unfinished business accumulates. Eventually they experience very intense, judgmental responses in the present which come out of their past. They are often unaware of these judgments, unrelated as they may be to what is going on in the moment.

These judgments, when they remain unprocessed, look like valid, reliable responses. In compulsion, 8/9/1s tend to trust them as real. For this reason 8/9/1s need to examine their "gut reactions." Are these genuine, or are they the result of a pattern of denial and repression?

> Someone I know says it this way: "I've ingested and digested my life, but I haven't assimilated it." Yes, I take things in and I feel them inside me contributing to what it is I'm feeling, but somehow they're just a lump in my stomach someplace. I don't move

beyond them or past them or learn out of them. They hang around and get in the way.

What this directee is trying to say is that the insights and connections, the observations and patterns that naturally flow out of past experience when it is properly attended to, are missing. Consequently, the movement and flow that testifies to perspective and freedom from past events does not take place. The individual is immobile—asleep or perceptually groggy with the heaviness of events whose significance has not fully been plumbed.

Feeling vs. *Judgment*

This tendency to feel certain, which 8/9/1s see as coming from the gut, but which is often really a blind sort of judgment, needs to be pointed out to directees in this space. It is true that they can have, at times, an almost uncanny accuracy about feelings genuinely present in the environment and those who people it. It is also true that they need to assess perceptions behind their feelings, to test them out against data. Are they responding to what is real or to a prejudice unconsciously formed out of unprocessed experience?

One of the judgments 8/9/1s make is around the issue of justice. Are they or others being dealt with according to the principles of equality? Does preference play a part, or is everybody involved receiving the same treatment?

> I was working my butt off trying to get equal working conditions for everybody in the office when I found out lots of people were happy the way they were. My issue, again. I could have asked them first and saved all that energy, but I never thought about it. Things seemed obviously unfair to me, but I guess not to some of them.

As 8/9/1s grow from compulsion to freedom, they learn to distinguish between justice and equality. Justice may demand that unequal distribution takes place, and 8/9/1 directors sometimes need to assist their directees to an awareness of the difference between everybody getting the same thing and everybody getting what is appropriate. A director's attitude of acceptance, of openness to directees as they are, can help discernment in this area. When their own personal needs are acknowledged and addressed, they can be more sensitive to those of others. As 8/9/1s are treated fairly but according to their unique person, they can often move to a multi-dimensional view of themselves and, consequently, of others. Meeting their prejudicial attitude without prejudice provides a boundary-free atmosphere. It creates an example of how to approach reality without pre-conceived notions.

Dealing With Feelings

Because 8/9/1s are prone to respond to life affectively, it is important for directors to possess and to convey an attitude of comfort with strong feeling. Directees who either habitually burst out in emotion or else have buried it so deep inside that when it does come out it is volcanic in its energy, can terrify themselves as well as other people. Such outbursts need to be handled with calm and assurance by directors who remain clear headed and unafraid when they occur. Directees who experience first the emotion and then in many cases guilt for having it, or fear of being overwhelmed by it, need such allowing presence.

As with other spaces, the way out is through these feelings. Somehow this needs to be conveyed to 8/9/1s. Feelings, after all, provide the energy for life's growing and developing. Strong as their feelings may be, the reality of them needs acceptance. When their directors convey this attitude, 8/9/1s are helped to greater confidence in— or at least resignation to—the necessity of paying attention to and dealing with their affectivity.

It needs to be noted that beneath the hard or tough feelings, which are frightening enough in themselves, lie the softer ones of tenderness, care, sadness, hurt, and whatever else renders 8/9/1s vulnerable. These stirrings are even more terrifying to 8/9/1s than their so-called strong ones, because they afford others information about where they can be "gotten." When others know where they are unprotected, 8/9/1s lose any advantage they might have thought they possessed.

People who are able to cause feeling responses, especially those they see as "weaker" ones, have power over them, something frightening for them to admit. All the ammunition is not in their arsenal; all the weapons are not in their camp. The back and forth of inter-relating becomes the only way to live. It must be based on trust in the other's care and integrity, or else they will come out the losers. In direction, as in the rest of life, this resistance, fear, and movement to surrender take place over and over.

> I hate to cry. It's not like I don't do it, but I really hate to do it in front of anybody. I don't like them to see when and where and how I'm weak. If I let myself cry with you here in one of these sessions, you can bet I trust you.

One effect of strong feelings is that people lose their ability to think while these emotions are being experienced. For 8/9/1s who so intensely feel, perception fades. Directors need to back away from processing such feelings while they are very strong. Questions leading to insight serve no purpose in the midst of such strong feeling. Directees in this space don't know, are not cognizant of, meaning, causality, explanation, evaluation, decision, and action at the time of such affect. Pushing them to struggle to make sense of things is frustrating and fruitless. Directors need to remember the questions that arise in those moments but to ask them later, after the feeling has subsided and reflection is possible.

Probably the most helpful response from directors is a quiet presence that conveys calm, acceptance, and encouragement to go on, into and through the feelings. An image of such an atmosphere in the direction relationship might be that of providing the directee with a large enough room in which to flail around. Such a place of containment would be like a room with a floor, walls, and ceiling carpeted so that neither the one who thrashes about nor others will be harmed. In such a safe direction situation resistance born of fear can lessen, and the essential energy to be found only in such emotion can fuel insight, choice, and action.

> One thing I've learned in direction is that there's no avoiding how I feel. It's like that kid's game of Lion Hunt. I can't go over, I can't go under, I can't go around. The only way is through, scary as that is. It's good to know I have my director there with me to guard me against myself.

The Issue of Power

Control and survival often blend for 8/9/1s. They respect people who are strong, and they test that strength in directors whom they need to see as people who know how to fight for life. Somehow, directors of 8/9/1s need to communicate at least two things: that they are not weaklings, and that they do not choose to make a fight out of the direction relationship. A sort of "spiritual hand-wrestling" needs to be unmasked as the distraction it is. Strength needs to be communicated instead as courage to address difficult realities.

One of the reasons 8/9/1s spar with directors, other than to find out the stuff they are made of, is to find out whether these directors truly are invested, whether they care about their 8/9/1 directees. Is this care brave and enduring enough to put up with the strong feelings that inevitably surface when 8/9/1s lower their guard? There are two sides to the preservation instinct in 8/9/1s. On the one hand they are careful to take care of their needs related to safety, shelter, and nourishment; on the other they sometimes disdain and dismiss these needs, neglecting themselves. Throughout this flip-flop from one extreme to the other, directors need to offer consistent presence that testifies to ongoing care.

The instinct of holding ground is part of the power issue for 8/9/1s. Unlike 2/3/4s, who adapt themselves to their environment, people in this stance adapt their environment to themselves. Eights tend to do this by domination: controlling conversations, conclusions, decisions. Nines hold ground more passively by planting themselves firmly and allowing no one to invade or make off with their turf. Ones operate on the environment, making it stronger, more perfect, more flawless. However it happens, 8/9/1s want respect for their power and strength. They also want to be able to respect their directors for not submitting to any power moves from them.

> I've really learned to respect my director, gentle though she seems. For a while I wondered what kind of stuff she was made of, but when push came to shove that's just what she was able to do! She held my nose in my stuff with that iron hand of hers in that velvet glove. I never doubted she was on my side through it all either.

Making and Losing Boundaries

They may look like they comfortably go it alone and seem ruggedly independent, but beneath this impression 8/9/1s ask themselves a confronting, frightening question: Who am I? The answer to this question addresses the 8/9/1 issue of boundaries and parameters. Where do I begin and others end? Where do I go when I am taken by passion? Will I lose myself if I allow this other person to come into my life? Will this other overwhelm me so that I have no more for me, no more of me? Will I make others and their issues and feelings so much my own that I have no boundaries anymore? These are a few of the essential questions, questions around their very being, which arise from fear. Such fear has to do with slipping from their firm footing and losing their ground. Self-reliant independence serves as protection while they grapple with what is going on and decide whether and how to allow themselves to be vulnerable.

The "top dog" quality sometimes experienced in 8/9/1s is aimed not only at controlling others but themselves as well. If they are harsh and demanding on the outside, they are also that way toward their inner child. Discovering this child, the more vulnerable part of themselves, and finding a sympathy toward it can be especially helpful for 8/9/1s, who have so many unfinished, unassimilated experiences of earlier times to resolve. As life continues, strength and toughness hide the fear of the 8. Cynicism covers the 9's childish innocence, while calm suppresses excitement. Hard work and striving deny the playful child inside the 1. Self-demand, self-neglect, and self-punishment are how people in this part of the enneagram get even with themselves.

It can be helpful for directors to point out where feelings play into the issue of power for 8/9/1s. One way directees in this stance show resistance to and maintain control of the direction relationship—and, therefore, of themselves— is through feeling. Some 8/9/1s blow up to show their strength and to scare the director away. Others shut down and refuse to let feelings show, often because they simply do not care to experience them. Directors may cower before emotional outbursts or get caught in continuing efforts to surface feelings after 8/9/1 directees have told them there are none. Whether it is conscious or not, such behavior assures 8/9/1s that they remain in the driver's seat and can frighten their directors or make them anxious. Either way, these directees are in a position to avoid the confronting and exhausting, yet invigorating and energizing, work of conversion.

Dealing with Opposites

The conversion task for 8/9/1s can be expressed in a number of ways. One of these is to move beyond struggle, to hold opposites instead of being caught in an endless either/or. To say this differently, 8/9/1s need to move to a place of perspective, separate enough from their experience to see both ends of it, as it were. This does not mean that they need to squash their feeling response to reality by detached, logical distance. Rather, it involves holding that feeling at enough distance to recognize they are different from and more than their affective response.

The struggle between opposites needs to be uncovered for what it often is: a way to avoid the genuine demands of the interior life and the commitment it calls for. As long as there remains a dichotomy, 8/9/1s can wrestle with alternatives. Such wrestling is a procrastination analogous to 5/6/7s' weighing of more and more possibilities before decision. Reconciling these opposites, synthesizing out of an instinctive thesis/antithesis approach, ends the battle. Creating a third solution involving parts of both alternatives helps them to resolution.

While getting past dichotomy removes obstacles to commitment, it also can suggest to 8/9/1s that they have not worked hard enough or fought passionately enough for the alternative they have chosen. They need to learn that sometimes what is not fought for can be trusted as a gift of life simply given. Living need not always be grappling with a series of dilemmas. Sometimes the Divine and people around flow together in a unified creation. The stance of cosmic struggle has been viewed in this image by an 8/9/1 directee:

> My view of life is of a gigantic fist shaken in God's face. God has the upper hand, but he's going to have to deal with mine and I'm a contender. Anything less than a fight between us would insult us both. Yet ultimately I know I'm going to lose. God after all does have the upper hand.

The issue of struggle shows up when 8/9/1s talk about their relationship with other people. They can be mystified at the response of others, who may consider them nonsupportive, abandoning, uncaring. In fact, 8/9/1s see themselves willingly giving others—spouses, children, employers, friends—what these people ask for. They expect people to speak up for what they want and need from them; they need to do so clearly and forthrightly. Without such a statement 8/9/1s sometimes assume, if they advert to it at all, that there exists no need for affective support or other kinds of help.

The fact that some people are not aware of or cannot clearly articulate needs is seen as simply the case; it does not indicate any need for a response from them. When it does happen that people are either too immature or unskilled to straightforwardly ask for what they want, misunderstandings often occur. 8/9/1s tend to feel that no expressed need exempts them from response. This is especially the case when they are experiencing intense needs of their own which outweigh, even drown out, what others may be asking for.

> My daughter keeps going back to the time when she was a kid and Joe and I were getting our divorce. She keeps saying I wasn't there for her, that I seemed not to care anything about her welfare, that sometimes I didn't even make supper or clean the house, let alone give her any attention. I remember nothing about those months except that it took all my energy just to get out of bed every morning. She didn't complain so I just forgot about her.

In spiritual direction, as in any close relationship, 8/9/1s need others to be present affectively as they deal with their struggles and put out their honest but unorganized bits and pieces. Setting priorities is often a problem for people in this part of the enneagram. Something akin to emotional brainstorming usually precedes any sifting and sorting of emotion. Not only do 8/9/1s value friendships in which they are free to put out their experience unreflectively and without order, but they find it necessary also to find a director who allows this to happen.

To the degree that the director can let things just hang out without moving to tidy up, pursue, organize, or prioritize experiences, that director will facilitate 8/9/1s' swimming with strong strokes in the sea of their unconscious.

Issues Around Anger

The first feeling 8/9/1s are usually aware of is anger. It is not that they find anger a pleasant or desirable emotion, but it is the one most familiar for many of them. In fact, in a compulsed state many 8/9/1s convert other emotions into anger, which they view as maintaining and manifesting strength.

The anger of 8s is usually aggressive. Nines are more apt to smolder quietly like gray embers, which only reveal their warm glow when blown on. Early on in an angry moment, 1s tell themselves either that their anger is justified and allowable so that things can be better, or else that it is bad and therefore should be dampened into resentment. Anger that is not owned gets projected onto the environment where 8/9/1s see others as picking fights, pushing against the boundaries they have set up, forcing them to improve. Since what they call anger may be only the surface feeling for 8/9/1s, one way to move people in this stance beyond a posture ready for battle is to note their body language and reflect this to them.

> I was telling my director that I expect to get my butt kicked in life. He pointed out to me how sad my eyes looked when I said that. I hadn't realized till he said that how much I hoped deep down somebody would come along who would just let me be the way I am, somebody who wasn't watching to take advantage of me, somebody who'd care.

All sorts of emotions are, of course, present and experienced by 8/9/1s as by everyone else. Another way to involve the body in awareness of and insight into a variety of feelings is for directors to encourage exaggeration of postures or movements they observe. A clenched jaw or

fist, a sigh or a tear, a shiver, when highlighted and perhaps identified with or dialogued with, can take directees
beyond a feeling to insight about the feeling. This is the
method of gestalt therapy, an approach especially helpful
to and probably developed by persons in this part of the
enneagram.

> My teeth were clenched and my director asked me to
> clench them even more. Then she told me to become
> my tight jaw and teeth and to squeeze out, if I could,
> what they were trying to hold in. It took some doing
> and some time, but I finally heard myself mumble,
> "Shut up and leave me alone." I knew I was talking
> to my mother. She had been dead for years, but at
> that moment she was right there in the room again.

Dealing with Intense Feelings

Because emotion can be so intensely highlighted in this
stance, it is sometimes helpful to make concrete feelings
that are global and pervasive. Then 8/9/1 directees are able
to note the actual data that led to their response. It may not
be that everyone hates them at all; perhaps they have
recently encountered a couple of people who do so and
now feel incensed or depressed as a result. Distinguishing
the facts from the feeling serves as a reality check. A proper
response to real situations is more likely when facts and
data are placed alongside undifferentiated, raw feeling.
Looking at the concrete also helps break experience into
steps or elements or pieces which, in turn, encourage insights. Once their minds can get around an experience,
8/9/1s are more able to recognize it and move into action.

Sometimes directors can help 8/9/1s come to more
accurate perception of their experience by asking direct
questions. This approach assists them to distinguish what
they felt from what actually happened. Such reminders of
reality lead to clarity and objectivity beyond pervasive
feeling. As said before, however, this questioning serves
little purpose in the height of emotion or the deadlock of
judgment.

Suggesting to 8/9/1s that they pay attention to their images and symbols and noting their similes and metaphors can help them perceive what is going on more accurately. Their tendency to analogical thinking, measuring one reality by relating it to another in comparison or contrast, can provide perspective, inter-relationship among ideas, and prioritization. Such analogy affords enough distance to move them into clarity and from that clarity to decision and action.

> I had a dream about paddling against the current and woke up exhausted. At work that day I got the same feeling, like everything was an uphill battle. Mixed metaphors, I guess, but you know what I mean. When I got home and closed the apartment door behind me, it was like coming ashore for a rest. I realized why I don't seem to want to go out much lately. I need my refuge.

Often their throw away, offhand remarks are not really so. These, too, directors need to pay attention to because they frequently are a cover for unacknowledged fear and the soft emotions 8/9/1s may be reluctant to admit. Directees in this space may be testing their director's level of listening and understanding by these out-of-the-corner-of-the-mouth statements or questions that seem irrelevant detours from the focus of a direction session.

> He kept asking me at the oddest moments whether I'd ever heard of this or that song. Did I know the words to it? I learned after a time that he was indirectly telling me what he felt by referring to songs that held those feelings. He couldn't put them into words—wouldn't put them into words.

Guilt for 8/9/1s is often around strong feelings of passion. Their intense lust for life can lead them to a feeling of self-indulgence and self-pampering. They sometimes consider themselves to be more animal than human. Eights and 1s communicate this passion overtly, although in differently nuanced energy. Nines, on the other hand,

defend against such emotion, pushing it down unconsciously so that they feel lazy, sometimes mindless, and
uncommitted. Either way, it is passion that tends to lead
8/9/1s to self-condemnation.

> I have a brass band inside me. Horns are blaring
> away and cymbals are crashing. It sounds like one
> of those crazy contemporary symphonies that's
> just a lot of noise. You can tell how I feel about
> modern music.

Directors who can wait until this wild cacophony quiets
down and the soft strings beneath it are heard are ones
8/9/1s learn to trust. Such directors do not frighten them
off. Courage to remain through irrational feeling testifies
to the wisdom, understanding, and fearlessness 8/9/1s
look for in a director.

Engagement in the Direction Relationship

Directors for 8/9/1 directees need to stay engaged and
to allow their directees to set their own agenda and assume
responsibility for insight and movement. Of course, this is
true for directors dealing with people in the other spaces
as well. Directors for 8/9/1s need to communicate that
they hope to facilitate movement in any way they can, but
that they do not intend to do the work for their directees.
Some 8/9/1s will read this message as a challenge not to
get lazy; for others it sounds like a welcome promise of
freedom from cloying intrusiveness.

While directors need to process along with their 8/9/1
directees, they need to avoid processing for them. They
can remain actively involved in a number of ways without
taking over what belongs to their directees. One of these
ways is by underscoring what their directees say, lifting it
up for their reflection. Noting patterns that are repeated is
another method; still another is indicating places of energy
they see to which 8/9/1s may be blinded because of
intensity of feeling. Reminding them of previous parts of
their story, either from years ago or a past direction ses-

sion, assists them to make connections where none may have been obvious before. These and other approaches can help 8/9/1 directees take hold of their experience and move with it.

One reality 8/9/1s are impatient with and get angry about is discomfort or disturbance. It is important that directors not try to rescue them from this dis-ease. Such pain and unrest is often necessary to push them out of their complacency. Smothering them with a kindness that blocks their pain by providing for their needs, helping them to forget their loneliness, and stroking their self-pity militates against growth. Nor does it foster respect. 8/9/1s are impressed by people who do not fall prey to any of the tricks they play on themselves or on other people.

Hanging in with them until they get into process encourages 8/9/1s to do the same for themselves. What is it that goes on during this waiting past a time of resistance? What occurs that keeps directors and directees mutually engaged without resulting in directors doing the work?

A director's summary of observations can encourage 8/9/1 directees either to fill in the gaps by adding details and examples or correcting misperceptions. In this exchange directees keep working by clarifying and further articulating their experience. Resistance on the director's part to be put off by sometimes abrasive bluntness testifies to involvement. Enduring the occasional insistence of 8/9/1 directees that they are experts on whatever is going on in their lives is another way to stay engaged. Such conversations are often designed to hold directors off and cover 8/9/1s' vulnerability. Directors need to see them as such. Refusing to argue with 8/9/1s and refusing to let them explain their feelings away put responsibility on them and raise a challenge without creating a battle. Doing so assures engagement without antagonism.

Questions can be helpful at times. Directors should avoid, however, interrogating 8/9/1s about how they feel and why they feel that way. Such questions can intensify their sense of feeling powerless, of not knowing their experience. It can also pull them out of what is going on and blur the focus they need. It may painfully cut into their vulnerability when they have lowered their defenses. They may not be able to hear such questions, let alone process them and respond. Once 8/9/1s learn to trust that their directors will not intrude, they will feel able to invite them in.

> This is my territory. If I want you there I'll tell you. When I figure out you won't force yourself in I just may ask you in, even though it's a mixed-up mess you're going to see. If I get any sense you'll try to get in my way and fix things, forget it. That's my job, after all.

In contrast to 5/6/7s, who need invitations to move out, 8/9/1 directees need the freedom to invite directors into their world; then they will do so. If they see their director as skilled in methodology but lacking in care, they will never offer that invitation. It is not the ability to work with them that engages 8/9/1 directees with their directors, but rather the sense that they matter to them as persons. It is hard to fool 8/9/1s into misreading skill as genuine sensitivity. When both skill and care are present, and after that has been carefully tested and verified, 8/9/1s find the direction relationship one of contemplative awareness and conversion.

CHAPTER 12

The 8 Directee

When 8s talk about their experience they often mention how intensely their energy affects them. Expressing, controlling, and channeling this energy become the focus of much of their direction. Sometimes this energy manifests itself in anger and aggression, but it might be more accurate to speak of it as passion for and commitment to whatever they are about and whomever they engage with.

Eights see life clearly; it is about survival. Because this is so, 8s grow up independent. They can go it alone, whether others approve or not. The important thing for them is to have integrity and to be master or mistress of self and the situations in which they find themselves. Early in life 8s learn the power of assertion. It is not that they consciously develop this sureness and strength; rather, they conclude, as they follow this instinct, that others respect them for honesty and the courage to fight for their beliefs.

Assertion can turn into aggression for 8s. This use of anger can be a tool for manipulation which 8s are willing to use, often for the sake of justice and right. Although it is not essential to win, 8s are careful not to lose in life. Anger is the emotion into which 8s are inclined to convert other feelings. They often grow up either as aggressive bullies or confronting challengers. As directors listen to their history, these themes of power and control emerge in a variety of ways.

Eights have a profound sense of honor and, as their compulsions lessen, make many selfless efforts for others.

It is not uncommon to find 8s in positions of leadership in education, politics, government, and religion. They can inspire energy as well as master their own as they move further along in the conversion process.

Eights hate what they consider phony and do not hesitate to address lack of integrity when they think it exists. In their efforts toward honesty and truth, however, they can get tunnel-visioned about what constitutes integrity. They pride themselves on being straightforward and faithful, and they abhor deviance and deception. This does not mean that they are deeply devoted to keeping rules, especially when regulations militate against equality and fairness. It is a sense of values that matters; should breaking rules preserve values, such behavior is justified.

Often idealistic, 8s believe in the triumph of justice. They disguise their native innocence with strength and often a certain toughness. Their humor can be heavy, cutting, and sarcastic, another form of protection from being taken advantage of. Directors of 8s need to help them distinguish between commitment and merely involving themselves in causes that leave them personally disengaged. When the oppressed and their oppressors do not have real faces, it can be easy for 8s to turn upholding what is right into ruthlessness.

> There's a story that captures a lot about who I am. They say an elephant was asked why he stamped on a little flea and crushed it. The elephant explained that he was only trying to trip it up. That's me when I get going on something vital to me. I can squash people who get in my way when all I wanted was to make them stumble—well, maybe fall on their face.

The other side of 8s, which they often see as contradictory to their strength and power, is vulnerability. They have a childlike gentleness, even tenderness. The word *magnanimous* fits the 8 who has opened out to others. Magnanimous means large-souled. The physical and psychic embrace of the free and non-defensive 8 holds a loving and uniting passion as overwhelming as their anger can be.

What turns 8s from being fighters to lovers? First of all they need to come to the conviction they cannot do it all alone. Mutuality and interdependence provide the nourishment that brings fruit to their labors. At the risk of being taken advantage of they need to learn not to hold out for their own ends, not to yield to fear of exposing their weakness.

While it is true that 8s can be innocent, they are not naive. Innocence means going into a situation openly, knowing what price one may have to pay. Naivete means not to know, not to see the implications of risk. Distinguishing between the two can help 8s hold the opposites of vulnerability and strength. At the same time as they know themselves to be alert and aware of danger, they also know they can choose to dare.

Emotions of 8s make an impact on others. They also make an impact on 8s themselves. Instinctive, gutsy, often gregarious, they reach for more and more of what feels good. They do not tolerate routine or boredom with much patience; in their frustration they move out for new and stimulating experience.

> I get tired of things quickly. That's why I kept changing jobs all my life. A new one is always better, so I'm not losing out, but once I've done the new one for a while I get tired of it, too. There's no more challenge. I feel like I'm cramped in so I push out again and find something new and more demanding.

One director commented on this 8 issue with this example:

> Alice puts a lot of time and money into one activity after another. The latest is yoga. She went out and bought all kinds of books to read about it and then researched classes and enrolled in one. She bought

special clothes and a mat to take to class. I commented that she'd probably be into something else in a few weeks. She looked embarrassed and then changed the subject. I figured I'd hit some nerve.

Excess can be an antidote for boredom, whether that is in the area of intellectual pursuits, work, socialization, entertainment, or the arts. Eights are prone to make trouble if the environment does not provide what they judge to be enough stimulation. On the other hand, while 8s find pleasure in losing their boundaries and flowing into situations and persons, they are genuinely fearful of this over-response. Emotion for them is not distinguished from their bodies. They do not "have" an emotion; they are what they feel. For that reason sensuality and sexuality are frightening to them. It gets them into trouble, makes them vulnerable to others, and pulls them down to the primitive and animal level.

Direction with 8s can be challenging. Directors need to be able to hold their own in a fight, whether this is an overt battle or one of wits. Personal honesty and integrity constitute the director's most significant measure of strength and equality in the eyes of the 8 directee. Once a director's straightforward frankness along with genuine care has been ascertained, 8s begin to let down defenses and reveal more of their delicate and tender feelings, their pain, sadness, and loneliness. Engagement with 8 directees is not boring, but challenging and stimulating, once they commit to the effort.

Eights appreciate support from their directors but are not interested in sentimental or maudlin expressions of it. Neither are they very enthusiastic over articulated compliments and affirmation. Directors who sensitively pick up honest experience testify to care.

Once a trusting atmosphere exists, 8s respond to the director's suggestions about how to gain insight. Unlike 2/3/4s, 8s do not get caught in self-analysis but move unself-consciously into active imagination, working with dream images, applying myth and symbol to their experience. As they become more free and less fearful they open to methods of interior work with the same gusto they display in other areas of living.

It is important for directors to give 8s rein once they touch into both memory and present experience. They need to explore and try out, to express feelings and articulate judgments. All of this energy, because it is so intensely felt, will frighten 8s; often they will project this fear onto directors, being tempted to hold their feeling back lest their directors not be strong enough to bear it. Perhaps here more than in any other space emotion needs to be let out, intense and frightening though it may be. Directors who fear such passion will slow down movement by aligning themselves with the fear in their 8 directees. They need to stand fearlessly before this passion so that their directees can also do so.

Strength but not aggression, power but not contest, honesty but not ruthlessness are what 8s look for in directors. In their personal journeys they need to move the focus away from battle and onto the pursuit of justice that offers a meaningful challenge for their energy. Justice is always embodied in personal, human situations. Because this is so, 8s need to develop respect for and learn to free their own inner captive. Doing this in their own conversion process makes them more sensitive to the inner captive in others. While 8s are likely to remain involved in causes, they need to learn to do so from the vantage point of mutual presence. Directors who encourage them to face the interior challenge of self-presence beyond self-judgment assist 8s to become people who empower others.

CHAPTER 13

The 9 Directee

When 9s are in compulsion they give off a settled kind of energy that is not so much peaceful as it is heavy and dead. Nines instinctively push down disturbing experience, especially related to confronting self or others. It is a sign to 9s, and to their directors, that something is trying to surface when life appears especially boring, tasteless, and without promise.

This is not to say that 9s are unfriendly, unwilling to interact, or disinterested in what is going on around them. They sometimes seem more engaged when this shutting down dynamic is operative. At times when they are avoiding getting stirred up interiorly they may socialize more than usual. They also may search for some stimulus other than human interaction. These distractions might be anything at all: intellectual pursuits, information collecting, workshops, courses, growth groups. Nines may involve themselves in puttering around with gadgets and machinery. They may become sports enthusiasts, often participating from the bleachers or before the television set rather than on the field.

This search for distraction to avoid embarking on the inner journey is a form of resistance that, despite the physical activity it may involve, has its roots in interior laziness. When 9s are still unenlightened, this dynamic probably testifies to the deeper, often unconscious, fear of stirring up large pieces of unprocessed history.

Perhaps more than any other people on the enneagram 9s want to hold onto the calm and safety of Paradise, that womb experience where all is quiet, needs are cared for, and nourishment is provided. With quiet resentment 9s want to recover what they see as their birthright. They spend much of their time when they are in compulsion resisting involving themselves in a world of interior and exterior conflict and confrontation.

The years pile up experience that has gone unattended, emotions that have not been worked through to freedom, disappointments that are unacknowledged. The pressure to hold down in the shadow an increasing store of ignored issues builds up. The tension this creates makes addressing them increasingly frightening and, therefore, difficult to undertake. Though they know at some level the journey must be their own to travel, they keep looking for someone or something to make it happen for them.

Often this quest is at an informational level: some course or teacher or workshop will give the answer. Eventually, if they go beyond thinking knowledge will solve things and enter into direction, they are inclined to depend on their director to bring about conversion for them.

This reliance of 9 directees can be a trap for them and for certain kinds of directors. Some directors assume the role of reversing the common 9 conviction that nobody cares. They respond enthusiastically to the happy reaction of their 9 directees over finding somebody to whom they do matter. Such directors may be inclined to assume responsibility for making these directees value themselves. Directors can be seduced into making the perceptual connections, pointing out insights, answering questions, suggesting discernment and decision methods, exploring options for action. Eventually they lose the respect of these 9 directees who, at a deeper level, know they have tricked their directors into assuming what is really their own personal responsibility for conversion.

One way for 9s to reduce conflict in their lives and still not get too deeply into change is to adapt themselves to circumstances just enough to make them endurable. Directors can play into this tendency toward minimal adjustment when they believe it signals radical change. Directors may back away from further confrontation thinking their 9 directees are confronting themselves. In reality, the discomfort when the director held them to their issues has been removed, while little interior activity has been initiated.

> I used to think we were getting somewhere in our sessions. There were occasional insights and admissions of self-deception on Mark's part. But the next time we'd meet it was as though the clouds that had parted had closed over again. He was back wandering in his usual haze, insulated from the realizations he'd come to.

Simply forgetting can be the easiest way to keep things calm and undisturbed. Not remembering stalls the conversion process. It also dispenses 9s from responsibilities of intimacy and friendship.

> Sam hit on something at a recent session that I could see absolutely terrified him. He got very pale and I even thought for a minute he might pass out. I had him in my mind all week. Would he be all right dealing with something so confronting all alone? Next time he came in he didn't mention the previous session. I waited for about ten minutes while he talked about other things. Then I couldn't stand it any longer, so I brought up the subject myself. He looked at me sort of confused for a minute. Then he said, "You know, I forgot all about that." I couldn't believe it! How could he have forgotten something so obviously significant? I've learned that's exactly what he does forget.

Interacting with compulsed 9s involves dealing with a number of passive aggressive dynamics. Their humor is cynical and off-hand and needs to be listened to for messages hidden in the thrown-away mumble. Often such oblique statements are a test of whether the director is paying attention and understanding. Anger leaks out in cool logic designed to trip up the other person.

Sometimes 9s slow down to avoid doing what people want them to do, waiting others out until they give up and go away. They can complain and whine or else go silent in a milder form of resistance. Most subtle of all is an attitude of apparent accommodation and a look of cooperation designed to get unwelcome people with unsettling observations—including directors—off their backs.

Decisions are often hard for even enlightened 9s to make. They may merely let ideas, feelings, and behaviors gather without setting priorities. In a dilemma 9s sometimes choose nothing. They settle for what is left over after other options either are rejected or become obsolete and irrelevant. It is hard for 9s to decide *for* something, because to do so means making a commitment. Once there is acceptance of personal responsibility, personal demands follow. It is also true that genuine commitment calls for passion, and 9s fear passion because it stirs them out of settled tranquility.

Although 9s may not act themselves, they do tend to sit in judgment on people who do. Because they feel disengaged they can dip in and out of experience and the conversations that grow up around it at will. They often appear and indeed do want to be friendly and nonthreatening. When their passive aggression riles people up and causes others to give up and go away, 9s often are surprised. They meant no harm; in fact, they may have very much enjoyed the other's company. But then, that's life, they tend to say; people come and go and you can't count on them.

When 9s get in touch with their dynamics they may become overwhelmed by the pervasiveness of their tendency to suffocate their emotions. What seems like a smothering blanket leaves them hardly breathing beneath it. When they do wake up, they can feel enormous guilt over refusing to fight for values and principles, over following the line of least resistance, over taking the cowardly way out. Such insights initially send them back into their emotional insulation. By this dynamic they once again distance themselves from the consequences of those realizations. Unconsciously they return to an inertia that either completely shuts them down or propels them into activities to protect from further awareness.

It can sometimes take much patience for 9s to face and address their subtle inner saboteur, who not only deceives others but themselves. Conflict, they must come to experience, can be at least worthwhile and at best enjoyable. It energizes. It infuses life with the meaning they fear does not exist. Conflict can resolve into a peace that is passionate rather than sleepy, unifying rather than boundary-creating. The environment from which they find it hard to distinguish themselves becomes an arena where their choices declare commitment.

While 4s take on the feelings of other people and their surroundings as their own, 9s tend to be absorbed in and merge with places and persons. When compulsive, this instinct makes them lose their identity in their surroundings and the people in them. As a virtue it fosters a profound oneness with creation, that unity and love which constitute the Good News.

Nines know they are called to prepare for such experience of surrender to life, to the Divine. Directors need to know it, too, and not help too much. Directors need to refrain from trying too hard to deliver 9s from their despair or struggle with them too devotedly for discernment. Rather, it is a director who cares for them even as he or she leaves them in their pain and insists that they make their own way who communicates the message 9s need to hear. Their directors need to be people who will not abandon them, but neither will they provide the nourishment for their journey. Only God will.

CHAPTER 14

The 1 Directee

The most distinctive quality of energy in 1s is their restless dissatisfaction. Such impatience extends beyond themselves to others and to situations in the wider world. They can hardly refrain from thinking and acting in terms of perfection. What will make things better? How can I avoid continual disappointment? How can I eliminate flaws, since anything flawed in thought, feeling, or action makes those ideas, emotions, and deeds worthless?

Ones are plagued with this world view. Out of it they are sometimes driven to criticize and reform. Their humor is often satirical, a purposeful sort of poking fun, usually containing some hope for amendment; in compulsion they really do believe perfection is possible. Their satire searches to find perspective on the foibles and sins of humanity that will eliminate, once and for all, what in compulsion they judge ought to be wiped out once and for all.

There is a drive in 1s toward a righteousness that carries heavy feelings of morality. This sense of what seems "right" to 1s differs from the "right" 6s talk about. For 6s the feeling is one of order, founded on rules and regulations to be sure, but with an emphasis on what is fitting (versus out of place) rather than the good 1s speak about (versus evil or bad). For 6s there is a correct side to be on in the issues of life; for 1s there exists one standard of moral perfection from which one must not deviate.

This interior attitude often manifests itself in serious intensity. Sometimes grim, 1s find it hard to play and frequently disguise their play as work in order to justify it both to themselves and others. They need to have more fun than they do, but they find it hard to take time for any play they do not feel they have earned. They must drive themselves, using time well in the important work of living a good life. In order not to waste time they sometimes overschedule themselves and come late for appointments, including direction sessions.

Obviously, the interior critic is a reality of great proportions in 1s. Every person is driven by an inner evaluator and judge. The emergence of this aspect of personality is part of everybody's story of ego-development. It might be helpful for those who are not 1s, once they come to know their own inner judge, to use their awareness as a help to understanding the 1 experience. Each person's history of grappling with being unacceptable can become a point of reference for what it is to inhabit 1s' interior world. Their assessor never sleeps, never forgives, always drives them to improve.

Sometimes, in pursuit of rest, 1s succeed in quieting down the critic's static and repeated accusations. The drivenness to perfection is projected outside, and other people are seen to be demanding and critical. Then 1s bounce back and forth. They accuse themselves first in order to avoid others' accusations; they defend themselves with explanations that justify their actions as moral and good or at least well-intended and as perfect as they are able to make them.

> I have a buzz saw in my head. My director commented the other day that while we were talking I was focusing my comments on a third somebody that I even seemed to be looking at while she and I talked. She waved at me at one point and said, "Hey, I'm over here. Who are you talking to?" It was that critic I was looking at, that part I know so well, always demanding justification for everything I think or do. I could almost see him. God knows I could hear him.

Of course, when 1s describe problems in relationship with other people, effects of this constant internal criticism become the focus. Because 1s feel impelled to address what others feel as brutal honesty but which 1s see as helpful confrontation, they are frequently experienced as antagonistic and aggressive. What they consider speaking out the truth often feels to others like a scolding. What they call urging others toward improvement can be experienced as annoying argument. What they judge as merely sharing their insights others may find intrusive. Interventions of this kind can become impediments to the flow of common work, group meetings, or personal conversations. What 1s innocently judge as inviting others to eliminate flaws, people on the other end of these exhortations consider statements of resentful disappointment.

From the other side of things, 1s often see other people as expecting too much from them. They feel they need to fight what they think are others' expectations, though these tend to be of their own creation. Ones can be touchy; they try hard, after all, and yet they seem not to get credit for doing so. People in authority, especially, may be seen as judging them wrongly, not appreciating them for their efforts. Here again the quality of relationship is affected by projection; the critic within becomes the critic outside.

At some point 1s need to stop fleeing from and cowering before this critical aspect of themselves. They must turn and stand and face the merciless judge who, like some hungry monster, never gets enough perfection to satisfy its appetite. Perhaps this confrontation can happen in active imagination, in which 1s are led through experiences where they actually do face and carry on a series of conversations with their accusing part.

However it happens, 1s need the support of the director so as not to lose perspective and slip into their former fear. They also need the director to encourage them to continue with their imaginative fantasy exercise should they think they are not doing it well enough. It is not easy for 1s to resist slipping back and handing over power to this judging aspect of themselves. It is important for conversion that they trust the deeper sense of being. It is at this source where goodness and life spring up that judgment ceases.

The director needs to align with the true self, with that part of the 1 which can admit that life is continuous growing and changing. They need to come to see that what is right for one person may not be so for another. However that realization happens, it always involves movement toward conversion, toward the genuine and unique word beneath the "good scout" persona created earlier in life.

Another aspect of 1s that flows from the first is their ambivalence concerning their primitive impulses. On the one hand, 1s would like to rebel, to break loose and disobey, to be promiscuous. On the other, they cannot allow this rebellion either in thought or action. They find it impossible to sin, hard even to conceive of doing so. To do evil would be to self-destruct. The result of this viewpoint is that they fear their instincts and try to subdue them by being rational and reasonable. In place of emotion and sensuality, which they feel they must curb, they impose rules of good moral conduct.

> I find myself saying, "How could I have been so stupid. How come I failed to do what I saw so clearly and knew how to make happen?" I just couldn't get it right, I guess. Someday I hope I can come to believe—no, experience—that "Gray is beautiful" in others, sure, but in myself, too, and even more importantly.

Somewhere along the way in direction 1s may turn their critical eye on the director, all the more the higher the pedestal on which they have set that person for admiration. It is important that the critics in both director and directee not form an alliance to destroy self-presence in the two of them. It is this acceptance of self that can facilitate conversion.

Gentleness toward self on the director's part is perhaps the strongest inspiration for 1 directees. It can help them see and experience the self-forgiveness that leads to love of self, others, and the Divine. It is just such humble openness to reality that constitutes human perfection. Self-acceptance then leads beyond to patience with their 1 directee, something so hard for that directee to find without someone's assistance.

> I've learned in direction that the most important thing in the spiritual life for me is to hang in there with myself. My director modeled that for me by believing in himself and in me and hoping in me and even more, by really loving me. I don't think I'd ever have learned what it really meant, let alone how to do it, without his example. In him I experienced what I think the acceptance of Jesus must be like and the life it can bring. That's what's important, not my endless demands that I be perfect. My director's not perfect and neither am I. But God is present when we're together. What else counts?

CHAPTER 15

The 8/9/1 Director

The themes and dynamics described in relationship to directees are, of course, present in 8/9/1 directors as well. These dynamics focus on both limitations and gifts, as do those of the other enneagram triads. This same distinction between compulsion and virtue must be made with 8/9/1s as with the other stances. Directors who are 8/9/1s sometimes respond blindly from their instincts. The greater their compulsion, the less able they are to see what is happening in their lives.

Once any persons have their compulsions unmasked and realize how these operate in their living, reactions become less blind and automatic. Eventually, for 8/9/1s and for everybody else, contemplative awareness reveals both native instincts and the compulsions that have developed out of and around them. When people become conscious of their situation they often want to try to fight against and wipe out the compulsive tendencies. And yet, efforts to eliminate compulsions cannot but attack the instincts beneath them as well.

While these steps occur for every person on the way to conversion and enlightenment, for directors and their directees they have particular applications. In the interest of refraining from inflicting their directees with their compulsions, directors can sometimes hold back their unique gift. The following discussion, as it has for the other triads, includes comments on how 8/9/1 directors find their exaggerated instincts affecting their direction relationships in blind, and, therefore, unconscious compulsion. It also warns of the trap that these same directors can fall into when they do become aware; that is, an effortful control which withholds the very contribution that is theirs to make.

Living and learning are probably the only ways to come to a balance between too much and too little. Hopefully, what follows articulates some of the problems that arise as life teaches us by trial and error. When directors recognize how they have first been blindly trapped by their compulsions and later trapped in efforts to eliminate those compulsions, they can gradually come to personal reconciliation with the instincts of their own space. Through allowing such consciousness of themselves and their history, change begins to happen. Awareness of the interplay among instinct, compulsion (vice), and gift (virtue) needs continual refinement in life. What follows is intended to assist this awareness for 8/9/1 directors.

The Problem of Prejudgment

If there is any accusation 8/9/1s find offensive it is that they are prejudiced. People in this triad pride themselves on wanting—and often working for—justice and equality for people. Living and letting live, even assisting wherever possible to assure a fair situation for others, is a constant theme.

Those who are not in this space, however, experience 8/9/1s many times as locking in on their view of what is right and good. There is good and bad, and the bad is to be found out and punished. Situations are appraised as right or wrong. People who do not see such situations as 8/9/1s see them are either unclear or are kidding themselves, covering over what really exists. This locking in on judgments can carry over to direction relationships.

> Doug was directing Matt and I was supervising. I could see Doug had concluded that Matt was angry at his wife. Doug was actively driving that idea home in a number of ways, hinting at it and even outright

> saying so. He wouldn't let Matt move on to where
> his insights and feelings were taking him, but kept
> bringing him back, as he said, "to face up to it."
> Maybe he was right, though I'm not even sure of that.
> I am sure, though, that he lost the flow of things for
> Matt in that session.

It often seems obvious to 8/9/1s what is going on with people and what others need to do to be honest. When this prejudgment occurs, directees may find that the session becomes an effort to explain their actual experience to their 8/9/1 directors rather than a pursuit of their personal truth. While it is true that 8/9/1s have a good instinct, an often accurate "gut response" to people and situations, it is also true that they, like everyone else, can be wrong. Awarenesses as well as the assumptions and conclusions around them are limited. It is important that 8/9/1s not deify what is surely a skill, though subject like all skills to human fallibility.

Sharing their perceptions of what is going on with directees can provide significant movement in a session, even when it proves to be an inaccurate or incomplete perception. Putting it out between them often helps directees to clarify and explain from their own vantage point. Articulating what directees may have been unaware of can lead them to deeper insight and feeling than they were previously able to acknowledge.

Keeping Perspective

In all of this, however, it is important that 8/9/1 directors remain open to the possibility of being completely, or at least partially, wrong in their assessment of their directees' experience. Directors in this triad need to be aware of the influence "feel" has in forming opinion and judgment and distinguish whose "feel" they are dealing with. Is it their own, or does it come out of the communication from their directee? Without openness to such considerations, 8/9/1 directors will find their sessions becoming sparring matches, if they continue at all.

This search for perspective is another constant theme for 8/9/1s . It shows up, of course, in their ministry as spiritual directors. A patient, intuitive stance results from their standing back a little to gain a panoramic view of past, present, and future, of feeling as distinct from being. To do so helps toward an attitude of ongoing process rather than now-is-all-there-is.

> I got lost in her pain. Just lost. I wanted to take her out of it somehow. Then she did just that. She reminded herself of what a good life she and Brian had had all those years they were together. I could see a flicker of hope on her face and I felt it, too. It was like we both came back from despair.

Such perspective is more than logical detachment. Rather, it is a wisdom infused with feeling and something 8/9/1s come to in conversion. Their objectivity always contains an emotional component because it flows through, even though beyond, a feeling reaction. They may not see this way of knowing as ideal; they might prefer a logical approach. Eventually, however, they come to admit, if they are honest, that theirs will never be that kind of emotionless perception.

The Feeling Function and 8/9/1 Directors

Because 8/9/1s tend to overuse their affective function, they constantly spend energy dealing with it. Whether they get blown away or worn out by feeling, or are involved in trying to shut it down, affect remains a constant theme throughout life. The strength of feeling reaction not only influences 8/9/1s as directors, but it has ramifications for their directees as well.

Directees who are uncomfortable with feelings, especially angry feelings, can be overwhelmed or frightened when they pick up their director's strong response. Sometimes, when they cannot acknowledge it in themselves, 8/9/1 directors project their own strong aggression onto their directees, whom they then judge to be angry. When this happens they may accuse these directees of picking fights with them even though, in fact, they may not be doing so. Struggles between director and directee sometimes follow from such situations.

Perhaps a more subtle manifestation of their strong emotional reaction occurs when 8/9/1 directors attribute to directees the feelings that rise up in themselves. When 8/9/1 directors are caught into and genuinely engaged in the relationship, what their directees say often stirs their own response. This is one example of how boundaries melt away and 8/9/1s merge with another person. The director's own anger or fear or sadness, stimulated by what the directee is saying, may dissolve boundaries so that it is no longer clear whose feelings are present. In such situations 8/9/1 directors find that, at least temporarily, they are unable to deal with their directees' issues, so involved have they become in the emotional climate of the session.

> I was supervising a session the other day where Jan said she'd decided to face how scared she was rather than run away into her usual intellectualizing. Sam, her director, who had been waiting for weeks for something like this to happen, picked up her fear as she began to get into it. I couldn't believe what I was seeing. He got so scared that he began to warn her to try to get some distance from her fear, some perspective on it. Jan kept insisting she wanted and needed to give in to the fear, that she'd been looking for courage to do that for a long time. The session turned into a back and forth between Sam's warnings to be careful and Jan's frustration over being urged out of her fear. They completely missed each other.

Dealing with Aggression

Aggression in 8/9/1 directors, and in those from other triads as well, can lead them to be hard on their directees. The theme of sado-masochism, punishment turned both out onto others and in toward self, is a common manifestation of aggression in this triad. One way it comes out is in directors saying what they judge they must say for their directees' good. Their confrontation may include statements about the importance of being tough enough to face things on the road to greater integrity.

> I'm saying this because it's what I'd want somebody to say to me. It's an honesty I want to give myself, so I'm leveling with you and offering you what I'd want. I know you can take it, and out of respect for you I'm putting it out straight. It may hurt, but there's no other way to grow in life. And I trust you want to grow.

Besides having its source in self-punishment, this harshness sometimes comes from pride in their courage to face hard truths. It is true that 8/9/1s, even without any intention to be so, are often very direct, even baldly cutting, in their remarks. When this approach is tempered by compassion they can, indeed, become masters of free and natural confrontation.

It has already been pointed out that emotion is where our energy comes from. When 8/9/1s feel the intensity of their emotions they can be impressive people to deal with. This strength can be a supportive and empowering one, encouraging directees to take hold of themselves and their circumstances in healthy, assertive ways. But at times it may be intimidating, either a direct or indirect force with which directees need to contend.

Life Viewed as Struggle

When 8/9/1s are more compulsed, they create an atmosphere of struggle in their direction relationships. They communicate that the issue of who has control is the important one, and they will not allow their directees to manipulate them. Directees can sometimes feel that 8/9/1 directors are trying to break down their resistance either in a passive or active way. They pick up that they are viewed in some way as antagonists by their directors, whom they experience, sometimes accurately, as being out to get the upper hand.

Some 8/9/1s distrust people who do not fight. As directors they may instinctively stir up conflict if none seems to exist to begin with. When directees eventually respond angrily to these efforts out of frustration and irritation, such compulsed directors then congratulate themselves on having been right, having held out for the real response. See, they argue, the directee really was angry but would not or could not admit it. Directees may go away from such experiences in desperation over being misunderstood, accepting their director's implied assessment that they are cowardly wimps, people unwilling or unable to face their aggression or else convinced they are superficial and unaware.

The more positive side of viewing life as struggle is that 8/9/1 directors often really can sense the presence of angry feelings when directees cannot. Being held to looking at whether anger or other strong feelings are present can keep directees from wandering off into reporting, reminiscing, intellectualizing, or some other avoidance technique. When 8/9/1 directors use their power to help directees stay in touch with their truth, they provide valuable assistance toward conversion.

> At the risk of pushing too hard I kept asking Steve if he was angry at his wife. He said he wasn't, but then while we were working on a dream of his he touched into his rage at her and at "life," he called it, which had let him grow up so naive that he'd been taken in by her manipulation. When our meeting ended he said how much pressure he'd felt from me and how he'd resented it at first, but that without it probably nothing would have happened.

Another aspect of their strength is that 8/9/1s are often champions of the underdog. As directors, their power and energy can help directees to find and own their own. When they are compulsed, however, it can lead them to see their directees as victims, when they really may not be so. The 8/9/1s' view that people are being unjust and unfair may perpetuate the same attitude in those directees who find comfort in hanging onto the role of victim. Such a situation allows 8/9/1 directors to fight not only their own battles but their directees' battles, too.

Empowerment

When 8/9/1 directors become more conscious and contemplative, honest and self-aware, they have much to offer directees in the way of companionship. They are not inclined to be possessive of their directees or to run their lives for them. Instead, they encourage others to assume responsibility and make a difference for themselves in their own lives.

Directors in this space tend to go into sessions without scripts, bringing presence rather than methodology to the encounter. When enlightened, they are less likely to be distracted from the meeting at hand by their own unfinished emotional business. Neither are they inclined to move into fantasies and plans around what they are going to do when their directee has left the room. When engaged in the now, neither bored nor detached, they bring a wholesome disinterest that is far from the lack of interest they communicate when they are compulsively tied up with their own needs.

Instead, they are awake and present to their directees. They are not stuck in their own unprocessed, past experience, but flowing with available, free emotion. The sleepy, dreamy attitude of someone compulsively distracted either with other concerns or with looking to have no concerns at all is not operative. It is replaced by strength and engagement. The strong emotion they grapple with in themselves is allowed and welcomed, even as it is not demanded, from their directees. They no longer yield to fear of being overwhelmed and made vulnerable. Such ease with feelings invites directees to allow their own emotion in a way insistence and demand never could.

Communicating Strength

When 8/9/1 directors are self-present there is a rock-like quality in them. Their bodies communicate an energy of being centered, relaxed, and open, unafraid of their own historical and current reality. When they care for themselves rather than beat on themselves with accusations and punishment, they are able to manifest similar care to directees. While they do not tend to be demonstrative, neither are they so laid back that directees wonder whether they have any personal involvement or concern for them. As they become more free, 8/9/1 directors make clear, straightforward efforts to let directees know of their desire to support them. Their vulnerability shows in an easy revelation of feeling.

Support from 8/9/1 directors frequently comes in the form of challenge. As conversion deepens for them they get better at challenging with sensitivity. By the time they have moved beyond both their own blind compulsion to be harsh and their self-accusing fear over their own strength, they are able to meet directees honestly. They do this with an ease and without excessive fear of complications that being direct may cause. They exchange engagement for the laziness they might have been tempted to, a laziness that avoids integrity. They begin willingly to expend energy around their directees' growth, accepting the effort this may demand in sometimes confronting communication.

Symbols and Images

Because images and symbols are so helpful for 8/9/1s in their own journey, they frequently invoke this approach toward self-awareness when working with others. They know how their own feelings can be stirred by this kind of interior method; they experience how it helps to find some shape and form for emotions. To say it another way, they know the power of imagery to help understand and express themselves. They learn that they need to ground what may seem amorphous and vague affectivity. Imagery helps them do so.

The freer they become in themselves, the more confidence and facility they have in helping directees confront and address their own experience through methods such as dream work, gestalt techniques, working with story and myth, and artistic expression.

> I asked her what her favorite fairy tale was and it proved to be an opening into lots of stuff. I remember when I first realized what The Ugly Duckling meant for me. I remembered how when I was a kid I used to sit and sob all by myself every time I read that story. I had to keep rereading it over and over for some reason. The reason was, of course, that it was about my own life. Now I see that.

Other 8/9/1s especially benefit from the modeling in this regard by their enlightened 8/9/1 directors. Directors from this triad need to remember that 2/3/4 directees may look like they are finding work with image, symbol, and myth helpful when really they may not be. Directees in that triad may appear to be moving interiorly with their images when, in fact, they are only conforming and carrying out suggestions from their directors. Rather than experiencing what these methods are intended to facilitate, 2/3/4s—unknown even to themselves—may only be going through motions, trying to cooperate in the direction session. As far as 5/6/7 directees are concerned, work with image and symbol may remain on a perceptual level as mere mental exercise. Their many words and ideas around images may look like an engagement that is actually not present. Again, they themselves may not know that they are caught in their hyperperceptive compulsion. It is important for 8/9/1 directors to stay alert for indications of insight and movement in their directees rather than to assume this approach is irresistible when it is taken up.

For 8/9/1 directors, either of these responses would be foreign. Once 8/9/1s determine to yield to the power of imagery they are swept into it. They know how significantly they can be touched by symbolic experience. Because this is true in their own lives, they may innocently assume it is what happens for other people as well. They may hold directees to work with images and symbols that has proven helpful to them. They may even see their role as directors to keep directees on this approach, insisting it is the way to affective response.

In fact, what facilitates 8/9/1 directors may trap people in other triads into over-actively working on images or hyperperceptively trying to figure them out. In short, their way may not be their directees' way, something all directors need to learn. In fact, probably nothing is more certain to keep the desired response from taking place than pressured insistence on a director's part that directees pursue what has proven helpful for the director.

Intense Feeling and Perspective

It is said that people teach best what it is hardest for them to learn. For this reason 8/9/1 directors, who cannot deny their own strong feelings, are often helpful working with directees who need ways to address theirs. Those directors, frequently 9s, who tend to deny their affect, can be helpful with directees who do the same or who are from other triads where the feeling function is not so strong.

Because 8/9/1 directors struggle to find perspective in either a morass of feeling or a desert created by trying to eliminate it, they are often skilled in helping others to find that same perspective. Lack of perspective is what leads directors in this triad to lose their boundaries and to blend into the feeling climate of another person. When this happens 8/9/1 directors often fail to distinguish their own feelings from those of others. As one has put it:

> I was sitting there with Marge and guiding her through an active imagination. The image she had of being imprisoned inside her skin just blew me away. I could feel that suffocating sense right through my own body. After we'd worked with this for about an hour or so I came up for air to find that she was sitting opposite me never having really been touched at all by what had wiped me out for a time. I guess all I can say is that it sure was an insightful and moving time for me. It didn't help her much, though.

Enlightened 8/9/1 directors learn along the way of conversion what helps them see the moment in a larger context. They learn how to include their perceptual function, in other words, how to arrive at a more connected, interrelated view of past, present, and future reality. They can distinguish their issues and feelings from those of other people. They are able to sift these for themselves and help directees to do the same.

Conclusions from Personal Work

Along the way to finding their own self-definition, 8/9/1 directors often work analogically with simile, metaphor, and imagery. The practice of dis- and self-identification, guided fantasy, graphic art, or simply talking things through with another often help in this process. Movement, mime, yoga, jogging, and other physical activities also help 8/9/1s gain perspective. As 8/9/1 directors grow in the ability to move easily with these methods, they naturally are led to suggest them to others. Initially, their own greatest enemy in personal conversion is resistance to embarking on them in the first place. Along their spiritual journey they may feel silly or stupid working with symbol and images. Often this initial reluctance in 8/9/1s stems from the fear of vulnerability or weakness they might experience as they move with these methods. Once this resistance has been put to rest and they jump in, as it were, they take to these approaches like ducks to water. It is no wonder they hesitated on the bank; they are easily swept away when they do surrender.

When 8/9/1s become directors, they need to remember that others may not be resistant at all to the idea of such approaches to the interior life. Many people are enthusiastic about the idea of working with perceptual and bodily imagery, and yet may not feel deeply touched by doing so. It is important that 8/9/1 directors not confuse willingness and cooperative interest in these approaches on the part of their directees with genuine involvement.

> One of my directees was into centering prayer methods. He spent an hour a day "getting quiet" as he put it. Personally, I find centering prayer the best thing for me, but the effect on him felt really different. He'd end up either twisted up like a pretzel inside or else sound asleep. I decided to help him explore other ways to pray. Guess what he found? Standing under the shower. That's where he prayed best.

The Director's Own Emotional State

Directors in the 8/9/1 space need to have the freedom to cancel appointments when they know they are not capable of emotional presence to their directees. When they are personally in the midst of turmoil and are either trying to hold it down or else drowning in it, they cannot be present to someone else. All of their energy is spent grappling with their own feelings. It is probably best in such situations to refrain from doing anything at all; surely they need to refrain from trying to accompany another in direction. One directee reports this experience:

> I came in for my monthly meeting with John and we began to talk. He seemed so distant and detached, even a bit angry when I asked him for feedback on something I'd said. I wondered what I'd done. As I kept on talking I was also weighing everything I said as to what was wrong with it. Finally I just quit and started to cry. He seemed to come out of a daze at that point and asked me what was wrong. When I

told him, he apologized and said it wasn't me at all, but something that had gotten to him earlier in the day. He'd wanted to call and cancel, but he knew I'd already left home so he had decided to stick with our appointment. Was I ever relieved!

Continuing with another in moments of deep feeling can actually increase the receptivity of directors in other triads at times. This is rarely the case for 8/9/1s, who are pulled into the undertow of feeling and need all of their energies to keep from drowning. Instead of sensitizing them to others, such a situation makes 8/9/1s inaccessible.

As one 8/9/1 director said: "When I'm hot, I'm hot; when I'm not, I'm not." When 8/9/1s are awake, present, engaged, and energized, their passion and compassion are palpable. When they are out of touch with their own experience and that of others, they are totally so. No pretense is possible; no show of involvement is even mildly convincing.

We see here once again the integrity of the 8/9/1s. What happens on the inside manifests on the outside. People always know where they stand with 8/9/1 directors, whether they say it in words or not. When they are consistently engaged in their conversion process, when they no longer blow alternately hot and cold about their commitments, they inspire trust and confidence in their directees.

The natural gift that 8/9/1 directors offer directees is to be totally present to them. While this ability can trap these directors into forgetting past and future, it need not do so. While such total involvement in the moment can make boundaries between persons dissolve, this happens only in compulsion. Their valuable contribution to others' process exists beneath either danger. It is experienced by directees as permission to let in and fully attend to all that the moment holds.

CHAPTER 16

Afterthoughts

> It is true to say that for me sanctity consists in being myself and for you sanctity consists in being *your* self and that, in the last analysis, your sanctity will never be mine and mine will never be yours, except in the communism of charity and grace.
>
> Thomas Merton
> *Seeds of Contemplation*

As I come to the end of this book I am aware of how many things I have tried to say. I am also aware of how little has been covered in this discussion of spiritual direction and other enneagram interactions. On the one hand, I may have been more definitive than I intended to be as I described various dynamics and how they intertwine. On the other, I wonder whether I have couched conclusions too tentatively out of a reluctance to speak in an overly definitive manner. Speaking about the mystery of the human person demands both accuracy and reverence.

One thing that has remained constant throughout this book is my fidelity to what I have personally discovered by observing, listening to, and relating with people around the enneagram spaces. I do these things from one vantage point with its limitations and distortions. I do so out of my personal compulsions formed around the instinct that is mine. I know I may have heard words that I translated into something for me which the speaker never intended to communicate. Such is one of the problems of being human. My consolation is that these very limitations serve to illustrate a basic enneagram theory: we will always filter experience out of our stance in life.

It is also true that, were this book to be written a year from now rather than at this time, more information as well as more sifting of my own life experience would make it clearer and more precise. This affords me with yet another opportunity to invite others into the process of developing and refining what constitutes enneagram study.

The challenge of companioning is mirrored in these pages, not only by what I describe, but by the fact that some of you will say, "No, it's not quite that way," or "It's not that way at all." May such comments stimulate more nuancing of enneagram dynamics, something that needs to happen always in enneagram development. I believe wisdom results from this correcting, explaining, and finding better words to say things not only here but also in spiritual direction and other relationship.

There is a risk in writing down what has been, is now, and always will be an oral tradition in the best sense. The enneagram keeps possibilities for learning open. It leaves conclusions tentative and subject to revision and refinement. It necessitates translation. Most of all, it draws those who are involved in its study to a place beneath the words. Once these words are put on pages, they may lose not only vitality, but also some urgency to explore further. I hope this is not the case with what you read in this book.

The enneagram defies the printed page. Its learnings come from the experience of energy within people. These energies early in life compulsively pull up and lock into the head place for 5/6/7s, the skeleton of the torso for 2/3/4s, the soft, pliable organs beneath that skeleton for 8/9/1s. As conversion continues, these compulsive energies fall beneath the diaphragm and become the centered energy of the *hara*, the gut. Even centered energy is different for each of the spaces. Besides the fact that it differs in itself, it is picked up by other people, themselves instinctively different. The readings and misreadings we have of one another can be traced to our varied energies and translation of others' energies.

It is centered life and the distinctive modifications of that centeredness that the enneagram attempts to describe. Such experience of the energies of life becomes more real as we continue on the way of conversion. When we do come to know this human life, we touch into Life beyond, above, beneath—however we imagine that to be.

In some ways the enneagram cannot be grasped at all. Who can hold the spirit/Spirit who breathes at will? Still, we keep trying to do so as human beings. At our best we are not attempting to pin down this spirit/Spirit. We only wish to know and feel and do more humanly. Those who involve themselves in enneagram study can get lost in the complexities of it. They can realize that, no sooner have they said something they believe to be so, than someone comes along with an exception or modification that proves them wrong. Such is the way of research, even descriptive research, about human beings. The spirit/Spirit cannot be contained; rather that spirit/Spirit leads us on to broader and deeper awarenesses.

Having written all this, I still offer you these pages, confident there is truth here. The observations flow from years of self-remembering, self-observing, and, I hope, self-understanding.

But I know they are far from the last word. The enneagram conversation, the descriptive research of this oral tradition, continues.

Resources

Assagioli, Roberto. 1974. *The Act of Will*. Baltimore: Penguin Books.

Campbell, Joseph. 1949. *The Hero with a Thousand Faces*. Princeton, New Jersey: Princeton University Press.

Corcoran, Sister Donald, OSB. 1982. "The Spiritual Guide: Midwife of the Higher Spiritual Self." In *Abba: Guides to Wholeness and Holiness East and West*, ed. John Sommerfeldt. Kalamazoo, Michigan: Cistercian Publications.

Gendlin, Eugene. 1978. *Focusing*. New York: Everest House.

Hillman, James. 1975. *Re-Visioning Psychology*. San Francisco: Harper and Row.

Malone, Thomas P. 1976. "The Christian Sacred Tradition and Psychotherapy." In *On the Way to Self-Knowledge*, eds. Jacob Needleman and Dennis Lewis. New York: Alfred A. Knopf.

May, Gerald. 1988. *Addiction and Grace*. San Francisco: Harper and Row.

May, Rollo. 1991. *The Cry for Myth*. New York: W.W. Norton.

Merton, Thomas. 1949. *Seeds of Contemplation*. Norfolk, Connecticut: New Directions.

Ouspensky, P. D. 1977. *In Search of the Miraculous*. San Diego: Harcourt Brace Jovanovich.

Palmer, Helen. 1988. *The Enneagram, Understanding Yourself and the Others in Your Life*. San Francisco: Harper and Row.

Riso, Don Richard. 1987. *Personality Types*. Boston: Houghton Mifflin.

Zuercher, Suzanne, OSB. 1992. *Enneagram Spirituality: From Compulsion to Contemplation*. Notre Dame, Indiana: Ave Maria Press.